With the Guards' Brigade During the Boer War

With the Guards' Brigade During the Boer War

On Campaign from Bloemfontein
to Koomati Poort and Back

Edward P. Lowry

LEONAUR

With the Guards' Brigade During the Boer War: On Campaign from Bloemfontein to Koomati Poort and Back
by Edward P. Lowry

Originally published in 1902 under the title
With the Guards' Brigade from Bloemfontein to Koomati Poort and Back

Leonaur is an imprint of Oakpast Ltd

ISBN: 978-1-84677-622-9 (hardcover)
ISBN: 978-1-84677-621-2 (softcover)

http://www.leonaur.com

Contents

To the officers, non-commissioned officers
and men of the Guards' Brigade

this imperfect record of their heroic daring,
and of their yet more heroic endurance
is respectfully dedicated,
in token of sincerest admiration,
and in grateful appreciation of numberless
courtesies received by one of their
fellow travellers and chaplains throughout the
Boer War of 1899-1902

Preface

The story of my long tramp with the Guards' Brigade was in part told through a series of letters that appeared in *The Methodist Recorder*, *The Methodist Times*, and other papers. The first portion of that series was republished in *Chaplains in Khaki*, as also extensive selections in *From Aldershot to Pretoria*. In this volume, therefore, to avoid needless repetition, the story begins with our triumphal occupation of Bloemfontein, and is continued till after the time of the breaking-up of the Guards' Brigade.

No one will expect from a chaplain a technical and critical account of the complicated military operations he witnessed at the seat of war. For that he has no qualifications. Nor, on the other hand, would it be quite satisfactory if he wrote only of what the chaplains and other Christian workers were themselves privileged to do in connection with the war. That would necessitate great sameness, if not great tameness. These pages are rather intended to set forth the many-sided life of our soldiers on active service, their privations and perils, their failings and their heroisms, their rare endurance, and in some cases their unfeigned piety; that all may see what manner of men they were who in so many instances laid down their lives in the defence of the empire; and amid what stupendous difficulties they endeavoured to do their duty.

We owe it to the fact that these men have volunteered in such numbers for military service that Britain alone of all European nations has thus far escaped the curse of the conscription. In that sense, therefore, they are the saviours and substitutes of the entire manhood of our nation. If they had not consented of their own accord to step into the breach, every able Englishman now at his desk, behind his counter, or toiling at his bench, must have run the risk of having had so to do. We owe to these men more than we have ever realised. It is but right, therefore, that more than ever they should henceforth live in an atmosphere of grateful kindliness, of Christian sympathy and effort.

God bless you, Tommy Atkins,
Here's your country's love to you!"

My authorities for the statements made in the introductory chapter are Fitzpatrick's *Pretoria from Within*, and Martineau's *Life of Sir Bartle Frere*. For the verifying or correcting of my own facts and figures, given later on, I have consulted Conan Doyle's *The Great Boer War*, Stott's *The Invasion of Natal*, and almost all other available literature relating to the subject.

Edward P. Lowry
Pretoria
March, 1902

The Ultimatum

When the late Emperor of the French was informed, on the eve of the Franco-German War, that not so much as a gaiter button would be found wanting if hostilities were at once commenced, soon all France found itself, with him, fatally deceived. But when the Transvaal Burghers boasted that they were "ready to give the British such a licking as they had never had before," it proved no idle vaunting. Whether the average Boer understood the real purpose for which he was called to arms seems doubtful; but his leaders made no secret of their intention to drive the hated Roineks into the sea, and to claim, as the notorious Bond frankly put it, "all South Africa for the Africanders." The Rev. Adrian Hoffmeyer of the Dutch Reformed Church freely admits that the watchword of the Western Boers was *"Tafelburg toc,"* that is, *To Table Mountain*; and that their commandant said to him, "We will not rest till our flag floats there."

Similarly on the eastern side it was their confident boast that presently they would be "eating fish and drinking coffee at seaside Durban." There would thus be one flag floating over all South Africa; and that flag not the Union Jack but its supplanter.

Now the Dutch have undoubtedly as absolute a right to dream dreams of wide dominion as we ourselves have; and this particular dream had no less undeniably been the chief delight of some among them for more than a decade twice told.

Even President Brand, of the Orange Free State, referring to Lord Carnarvon's pet idea of a federated South Africa, said: "His great scheme is a united South Africa *under the British flag*. He dreams of it and so do I; but *under the flag of South Africa.*" Much in the same strain President Burgers, of the Transvaal Republic, when addressing a meeting of his countrymen in Holland, said: "In that far-off country the inhabitants dream of a future in which the people of Holland will recover their former greatness." He was convinced that within half a century there would be in South Africa a population of eight millions; all speaking the Dutch language; a *second* Holland, as energetic and liberty-loving as the first; but greater in extent, and greater in power.

Nevertheless, in this far-seeing President's day, the Transvaal, after fourteen years of doubtful independence, reached in 1877 its lowest depths of financial and political impotency. Its valiant burghers were vanquished in one serious conflict with the natives; and, emboldened thereby, the Zulus were audaciously threatening to eat them up, when Shepstone appeared upon the scene.

"I thank my father Shepstone for his restraining message," said Cetewayo. "The Dutch have tired me out; and I intended to fight with them once, *only once*, and to drive them over the Vaal." The jails were thrown open because food was no longer obtainable for the prisoners. The State officials, including the President, knew not where to secure their stipends, and were hopelessly at variance among themselves. The Transvaal one-pound notes were selling for a single shilling, and the State treasury contained only twelve shillings and sixpence wherewith to pay the interest on a comparatively heavy State debt, besides almost innumerable other claims.

No wonder, therefore, that Burgers, in disgust, declared he would sooner be a policeman under a strong government. "Matters are as bad as they ever can be," said he; "they cannot be worse!" Hence its annexation, in 1877, by Sir Theophilus Shepstone, without the assistance of a solitary soldier, but with the eager assent of thousands of the burghers, bade fair to prove the salvation of the Transvaal, and probably would have done, had the easily-to-be-obtained consent of the *Volksraad* been at once sought, and Lord Carnarvon's promise of speedy South African Federation, together with a generous measure of local self-government, been promptly redeemed. But European complications, with serious troubles on the Indian frontier, caused interminable delay in the maturing of this scheme; and as the disappointed Boers grew restive, a *Hold Your Jaw Act* was passed, making it a penal offence for any Transvaaler even to discuss such questions. In our simplicity we sit upon the safety valve and then wonder why the boiler bursts. To the Hold Your Jaw policy the Boer reply was an appeal to arms; and at Majuba in the spring of 1881 their rifles said what their jaws were forbidden to say. Majuba was indeed a mere skirmish, an affair of outposts; but Magersfontein and Spion Kop are the legitimate sons of Majuba.

Napoleon, with possibly a veiled reference to himself, once said to the French people, "You have the men, but where is *the Man?*" The Boers in the day of their uprising against British rule found *the Man* in Paul Stephanus Kruger. To all South Africa a veritable *man of Destiny* has he proved to be; and for eighteen successive years, as their honoured President he has ruled his people with an absoluteness no European potentate could possibly approach. By birth a British subject, and for a brief while after the annexation a paid official of the British Government, he yet seems all his life to have been a consistent hater of all things British. When only ten years old, a tattered, bare-legged, unlettered lad, he joined *the great trek* which in 1837 sought on the dangerous and dreary *veldt* beyond the Vaal a refuge from British rule. He it was who, surviving the terrors of those tragic times and trained in that stern school, became like Brand and Burgers a dreamer of dreams. He lived to baffle by his superior shrewdness, or slimness, all the arts of English diplomacy. In his later years this President manifestly deemed himself chosen of Heaven to make an end of British rule from the Zambezi to the sea. "The Transvaal shall never be shut up in a kraal," said he. A Sovereign International State he declared it was, or should be, with free access to the ocean; and how astonishingly near he came to the accomplishment of these bold aims we now know to our exceeding cost. Nevertheless, to this persistent dreamer of dreams the two South African Republics owe their extinction; while the British Empire owes to him more than to any other living man its fast approaching Federation.

With surprising secrecy and success the Transvaal officials prepared for the inevitable conflict which the attempted fulfilment of such bold dreams involved, and in that preparation were rendered essential aid, first by the discovery, not far from Pretoria, of the richest goldfield in the whole world, which soon provided them with the necessary means; and next by the Jameson Raid, which provided them with the necessary excuse.

To Steevens, the lamented correspondent of *The Daily Mail*, a Dopper editor and predikant said, "I do not think the Transvaal Government has been wise, and I told them they made a great mistake when they let people come in to the mines. *This gold will ruin you; to remain independent you must remain poor*"! Perhaps so! but the modern world is not built that way. No trekkers nowadays may take possession of half a continent, forbid all others to come in, and right round the frontier post up notices "Trespassers will be prosecuted." Even Robinson Crusoe had not long landed on his desolate isle when he was startled by the sight of a strange footprint on the seashore sand. Welcome or unwelcome, somebody else had come! Crusoe and his man Friday might set up no exclusive rights in a heritage that for a brief while seemed all their own. The Boer with his *Kaffir* bondsman has been compelled to learn the same distasteful lesson. The wealth of the Witwaters Rand was for those who could win it; and for that stupendous task the Boer had neither the necessary aptitude nor the necessary capital. It was not, therefore, for him to echo the cry of Edie Ochiltree when he found hid treasure amid the ruins of St Roth's Abbey—"Nae halvers and quarters,—hale o' mine ain and nane o' my neighbours." The bankrupt Boer had to let his enterprising neighbour in to do the digging, or get no gold at all.

Nevertheless, the upspringing as by magic of the great city of Johannesburg in the midst of the dreary *veldt* filled Kruger's soul with loathing. When once asked to permit prospecting for minerals around Pretoria, he replied, "Look at Johannesburg! We have enough gold and gold seekers in the country already!"

The presence of this ever-growing multitude was felt to be a perpetual menace to Dutch, and more especially to Dopper supremacy. So, in his frankly confessed detestation of them, their Dopper President for five years at a stretch never once came near them, and when at last he ventured to halt within twenty miles of their great city it was thus he commenced his address to the crowd at Krugersdorp:—"Burghers, friends, *thieves, murderers, newcomers,* and others."

The reek of the Rand was evidently even then in his nostrils; and the medieval saint that could smell a heretic nine miles off was clearly akin to Kruger. Unfortunately for him the newcomers outnumbered the old by five to one, and were a bewilderingly mixed assortment, representing almost every nationality under the whole heaven. In what had suddenly become the chief city of the Transvaal, with a white population of over 50,000, only seven per cent. were Dutch, and sixty-five per cent. were British. These aliens from many lands paid nearly nine-tenths of the taxes, yet were persistently denied all voice alike in national and municipal affairs.

"Rights!" exclaimed the angry President when appealed to for redress, "Rights! They shall win them only over my dead body!"

At whatever cost he was stubbornly resolved that as long as he lived the tail should still wag the dog instead of the dog the tail; and that a continually dwindling minority of simple farmer folk should rule an ever-growing majority of enterprising city men. Though the political equality of all white inhabitants was the underlying condition on which self-government was restored to the Transvaal, what the Doppers had won by bullets they would run no risk of losing through the ballot box, and so one measure of exclusion after another rapidly became law. When reminded that in other countries Outlanders were welcomed and soon given the franchise, the shrewd old President replied, "Yes! but in other countries the newcomers do not *outswamp* the old burghers."

The whole grievance of the Boers is neatly summed up in that single sentence; and so far it proves them well entitled to our respectful pity.

It was, however, mere fatalism resisting fate when to a deputation of complaining Outlanders Kruger said "Cease holding public meetings! Go back and tell your people I will never give them anything!" Similarly when in 1894 35,000 adult male Outlanders humbly petitioned that they might be granted some small representation in the councils of the Republic, which would have made loyal burghers of them all, the short-sighted President contended that he might just as well haul down the Transvaal flag at once. There was a strong Dopper conviction that to grant the franchise on any terms to this alien crowd would speedily degrade the Transvaal into a mere Johannesburg Republic; and they would sooner face any fate than that; so the Raad, with shouts of derision, rejected the Outlanders' petition as a saucy request to commit political suicide. They felt no inclining that way! Nevertheless one of their number ventured to say, "Now our country is gone. Nothing can settle this but fighting!" And that man was a prophet.

For that fighting the President and his Hollander advisers began to prepare with a timeliness and thoroughness we can but admire, however much in due time we were made to smart thereby. Through the suicide of a certain State official it became known that in 1894—long therefore before the Raid—no less than £500,000 of Transvaal money had been sent to Europe for secret uses. Those secret uses, however, revealed themselves to us in due time at Magersfontein and Colenso. The Portuguese customs entries at Delagoa Bay will certify that from 1896 to 1898 at least 200,000 rifles passed through that port to the Transvaal. It was an unexampled reserve for states so small. The artillery, too, these peace-loving Boers laid up in store against the time to come, not only exceeded in quantity, but also *outranged*, all that British South Africa at that time possessed. Their theology might be slightly out-of-date, but in these more material things the Boers were distinctly up-to-date. For many a week after the war began both the largest and the smallest shells that went curving across our battlefields were theirs; while many of our guns were mere popguns firing smoky powder, and almost as useless as catapults. It was not a new raid these costly weapons were purchased to repel; neither men nor nations employ sledge-hammers to drive home tinned-tacks. It was a mighty

Empire they were intended to assail; and a mighty Republic they were intended to create.

When the fateful hour arrived for the hurling of the Ultimatum, in very deed "not a gaiter button" was found wanting on their side; and every fighting man was well within reach of his appointed post. Fierce-looking farmers from the remotest *veldt*, and sleek urban Hollanders, German artillerists, French generals, Irish-Americans, Colonial rebels, all were ready. The horse and his rider, prodigious supplies of food stuffs, and every conceivable variety of warlike stores, were planted at sundry strategic points along the Natal and Cape Colony frontiers. War then waited on a word and that word was soon spoken!

As early as September 18th, 1899, the Transvaal sent an unbending and defiant message to the British Government. On September 21st the Orange Free State, after forty years of closest friendship with England, officially resolved to cast in her lot with the Transvaal against England. On September 29th through railway communication between Natal and the Transvaal was stopped by order of the Transvaal Government. On September 30th twenty-six military trains left Pretoria and Johannesburg for the Natal border; and that same day saw 16,000 Boers thus early massed near Majuba Hill. Yet at that very time the British forces in South Africa were absolutely and absurdly inadequate not merely for defiance but even for defence. On October 3rd, a full week before the delivery of the Ultimatum, the Transvaal mail train to the Cape was stopped at the Transvaal frontier, and the English gold it carried, valued at £500,000, was seized by the Transvaal Government. Whether that capture be regarded merely as a premature act of war or as highway robbery, it leaves no room for doubt as to which side in this quarrel is the aggressor; and when at last the challenge came, even chaplains could with a clear conscience, though by no means with a light heart, set out for the seat of war.

Surely never since the world began was such an Ultimatum presented to one of the greatest Powers on earth by what were supposed to be two of the weakest. At the very time that armed and eager burghers were thus massing threateningly on our fron-

tiers, the Queen it will be remembered was haughtily commanded to withdraw from those frontiers the pitifully few troops then
guarding them; to recall, in the sight of all Europe, every soldier
that in the course of the previous twelvemonth had been sent to
our South African Colonies; and solemnly to pledge herself, at
Boer bidding, that those then on the sea should not be suffered
to set foot on African soil. Moreover, so urgent was this audacious
demand that Pretoria allowed London only forty-eight hours in
which to decide what should be its irrevocable doom, to lay aside
the pride of empire, or pay the price of it in blood.

Superb in its audacity was that demand: and, if war was indeed fated to come, this daring challenge was for England as
serviceable a deed as unwitting foemen ever wrought.

It put a sudden end for a season to all controversy. It rallied
in defence of our Imperial heritage almost every class, and every
creed. It thrilled us all, like the blast of the warrior horn of Ro-
derick Dhu, which transformed the very heather of the High-
lands into fighting men. As the soldiers' laureate puts it "Duke's
son and cook's son," with rival haste responded to the martial
call. To serve their assailed and sorrowing Queen, royal court
and rural cottage gave freely of their best. It intensified the patriotism of us all; and probably never, since the days of the Armada,
had the United Kingdom of Great Britain and Ireland found
itself so essentially united.

The effect of the Ultimatum throughout the length and breadth
of Greater Britain was no less remarkable than its first results at
home. Not only the two Colonies that, alas, were soon to be overrun by hostile hordes, and mercilessly looted, but also those far-
thest removed from the fray, instantly took fire, and burned with
imperialistic zeal that stinted neither men nor means.

"A varied host, from kindred realms they come, Brethren in
arms, but rivals in renown."

The declaration of war united the ends of the earth in a common enthusiasm, and sent a strange throb of brotherhood right
round the globe. The whole empire at last awoke to a sense of its
essential oneness. Australians and Canadians, men from Burma,
from India and Ceylon, speedily joined hands on the far distant

veldt in defence of what they proudly felt to be their heritage as well as ours. Their presence in the very forefront of the fray betokened the advent of a new era. Nobler looking men, or men of a nobler spirit, were never brought together at the unfurling of any banner. They were the outcome of competitions strangely keen and close. Sydney for instance called for five hundred volunteers; but within a few days *three thousand* five hundred valiant men were clamouring for acceptance. So was it in Montreal. So it was everywhere. Often too at no slight financial sacrifice was the post of peril sought. As a type of many more, I was told of an Australian doctor who paid a substitute £300 to carry on his practice, while he as a private joined the fighting ranks and faced cheerily the manifold privations of the hungry *veldt*. Rich is the empire that owns such sons; and myriads of them in the hour of impending conflict were ready to say—

War? We would rather peace!
But, mother, if fight we must,
There are none of your sons on whom you can lean with a surer trust.
Bone of your bone are we; and in death would be dust of your dust!

It was the Ultimatum that thus linked to each other and to us those loyal hearts that longed to keep the empire whole; and thus President Kruger in his blindness became Greater Britain's boundless benefactor.

CHAPTER 1

To Bloemfontein

For old times' sake
Don't let enmity live;
For old times' sake
Say you will forget and forgive.
Life is too short for quarrel;
Hearts are too precious to break;
Shake hands and let us be friends
For old times' sake!

So gaily sang the Scots Guards as, in hope of speedy triumph and return, we left Southampton for Kruger's Land on the afternoon of October 21st, 1899.

Our last evening in England brought us the welcome tidings that on that day, the Boers who had thus early invaded Natal with a view to annexing it, had been badly beaten at Talana Hill. That seemed a good beginning; and it sent us to sea with lightsome hearts; nor was it till long after we landed in South Africa that we learned what had really taken place during our cheerful voyage;—that on the very day we embarked, the battle of Elandslaagte had been won by our hard-pressed comrades, but at a cost of 260 casualties; and that the very next day—The *Nubia*'s first Sunday at sea—Dundee with all its stores had perforce been abandoned by 4000 of our retreating troops, for whose relief, two days later, Tinta Inyoni was fought by General French; that on Oct. 29th while we were spending a tranquil Sunday in St Vincent's harbour there

A Magersfontein Boer Trench

commenced the struggle that culminated in the Nicholson's
Nek disaster; and that on Nov. 13th, while we were awaiting orders in Table Bay, the capture of our armoured train at
Chieveley took place. Clearly it was blissful ignorance that
begat our hopes of brief absence from home, and of the easy
vanquishing of our hardy foes!

Two days later I reached the Orange River; and, on the courteous suggestion of Lord Methuen, was attached to the mess
of the 3rd Grenadier Guards, as was also my "guide, philoso-
pher and friend" the Rev. T. F. Falkner our Anglican chaplain.
Here I left my invaluable helper, Army Scripture Reader Pearce;
while, with the Guards' Brigade now made complete by the
arrival of the 1st and 2nd Coldstream battalions, I pushed forward to be present at the four battles which followed in startlingly swift succession, and which I have already with sufficient
fullness described in *Chaplains in Khaki, viz.* Belmont on Nov.
23rd, Graspan on Nov. 25th, Modder River on Nov. 28th, and
the Magersfontein defeat on Dec. 11th, for which, however, the
next Amajuba Day—Feb. 27th, 1900—brought us ample compensation in the surrender of Cronje and his 4000 veterans, with
the ever memorable sequel to that surrender, the occupation of
Bloemfontein by the British forces.

It would probably be difficult to find anywhere under the
sun a more prosperous and promising little city, or one better
governed than Bloemfontein, which the Guards entered on
the afternoon of Tuesday, March 13th, 1900. There is not a
scrap of cultivated land anywhere around it. It is very literally a
child of the *veldt*; and still clings strangely to its nursing mother.
Indeed the *veldt* is not only round about it on every side, but
even asserts its presence in many an unfinished street. You are
still on the *veldt* in the midst of the city; and the characteristic
kopje is in full view here, there, and everywhere. On one side
of the city is the old fort built by the British more than fifty
years ago, and soon after vacated by them, but it is erected of
course on a *kopje*, on one slope of which, part of the city now
stands. On the opposite side of the town is a new fort; but
that also crowns a *kopje*. This metropolis of what was then the

Orange Free State, thus intensely African in its situation and surroundings, was nevertheless an every way worthy centre of a worthy State.

Many of its public buildings are notably fine, as for instance the Government Offices over which it was my memorable privilege to see the Union Jack unceremoniously hoisted; and the Parliament Hall, on the opposite side of the same road, erected some twelve years ago at a cost of £80,000. The Grey College, which accommodates a hundred boy boarders, is an edifice of which almost any city would be proud; and The Volk's Hospital, that is The People's Hospital, is also an altogether admirable institution. From the commencement of the war this was used for the exclusive benefit of sick or wounded Boers and of captured Britishers who were in the same sore plight. Among these I found many English officers, who all bore witness to the kind and skilful treatment they had uniformly received from the hospital authorities; but when the Boer forces hurried away from Bloemfontein they were compelled to leave their sick and wounded behind; with the result that as at Jacobsdal, the English patients at once ceased to be prisoners, while the Boer patients at once became prisoners. So do the wheels of war and fortune go whirling round!

With a white population of under ten thousand all told, a large proportion is of British descent; and presently a positively surprising number of Union Jacks sprang forth from their hiding-places and fluttered merrily all over the town. Everybody was thankful that no bombardment had taken place; but many even of the British residents regarded with sincere regret the final extinction of the independence of this once self-governed and well-governed Republic.

The story has now everywhere been told of the soldier lad who, when he caught sight of his first swarm of locusts, wonderingly exclaimed as he noted their peculiar colour, "I'm blest if the butterflies out here haven't put on khaki."

Bloemfontein very soon did the same. Khaki of various shades and various degrees of dirtiness saluted me at every point. Khaki men upon khaki men swarmed everywhere. Brigade followed brigade in apparently endless succession; but all clad in the same irrepressible colour, till it became quite depressing. No wonder the townspeople soon took to calling the soldiers *locusts*, not merely out of compliment to the gay colour of their costume, but also as aptly descriptive of their apparent countlessness. They seemed like the sands by the seashore, innumerable. They bade fair to swallow up the place.

That last expression, however, suggests yet another point of resemblance. For longer than these men seemed able to remember, the order of the day had been *long marches and short rations.* When, therefore, they reached this welcome halting-place they were simply famished; insatiably hungry, they eagerly spent their last coin in buying up whatever provisions had fortunately escaped the commandeering of the Boers. There was no looting, no lawlessness of any kind; and many a civilian gave his last loaf to a starving trooper. There was soon a famine in the place and no train to bring us fresh supplies. All the bakeries of the town were commandeered by the new government for the benefit of the troops; but like the five loaves of the gospel story, "What were they among so many?" I saw the men, like swarms of bees, clustering around the doors and clambering on to the window-sills of these establishments, enjoying apparently the smell of the baking bread, and cherishing the vain hope of being able to purchase a loaf when at last the ovens were emptied.

So too at the grocers' shops, a *tail* was daily formed outside the door, which at intervals was cautiously opened to let in a few at a time of these clamorous customers, who presently retired by the back door, laden more or less with such articles as happened to be still in store; but muttering as they came out "this is like Klondyke," with evident reference not to Klondyke gold, but to Klondyke prices. It was not the traders that needed protection as against the troopers, but the troopers that needed protection as against some of the traders. Even proclamation prices were alarmingly high, as for instance, a shilling for a pound of sugar. Sixpence was the popular price for a cup of tea, often without milk or sugar. The quartermaster whose tent I shared was charged four shillings for a single whisky and soda, and was informed that if he wanted a bottle of whisky the price would be thirty-five shillings. On such terms tradesmen who, before the war, had laid in large and semi-secret stores now reaped a magnificent harvest. One provision merchant was reported to have thus sold £700 worth of goods before breakfast on a certain Saturday morning, in which case he would perhaps reckon that on that particular date his breakfast had been well earned. It probably meant in part a wholesale army order; but even in that case it would be for cash, and not a case of commandeering after the fashion of the Boers.

A crippled Scandinavian tailor told me that his constant charge, whether to Colonels or *Kaffirs*, was two shillings an hour; and that he thought his needle served him badly if it did not bring him in £6 a week. About the same time a single-handed but nimble-fingered barber claimed to have made £100 in one week out of the invading British; but his victims declared that his price was a shilling for a shave and two shillings for a clip. At those figures the seemingly impossible comes to pass—if only customers are plentiful enough. Oh for a business in Bloemfontein!

The Republicans of South Africa have always been credited with an ingrained objection to paying rates and taxes even in war time; but they frankly recognise the reasonableness of governmental commandeering, and apparently submit to it without a murmur; especially when it hits most heavily the stranger within their gates. Accordingly, the war-law of the Orange Free State authorises the commandeering without payment of every available man, and of all available material of whatsoever kind within thirty days of war being declared. During those thirty days, therefore, the war-broom sweeps with a most commendable thoroughness; and all the more so, because after that date everything must be paid for at market values. Why pay, if being a little *previous* will serve the same purpose?

A gentleman farmer whom it was my privilege to visit, some fifteen miles out from Bloemfontein, told me he had been thus commandeered to the extent of about £3100; the value of wagons, oxen, and produce, he was compelled gratuitously to supply to his non-taxing government. A specially prosperous storekeeper in the town was said to have had £600 worth of goods taken from him in the same way; but then, of course, he had the compensating comfort of feeling that he was not being taxed! Even Republics cannot make war quite without cost; and by this time some are beginning to discover that it is the most ruinously expensive of all pursuits.

The Republican conscription was equally wide reaching; for every capable man between the ages of sixteen and sixty was required to place himself and his rifle at the service of the State. Even sons of British parentage, being burghers, were not allowed to cross the border and so escape this, in many a case, hateful obligation. Their life was forfeit, if they sought to evade the dread duties of the fighting line, and refused to level reluctant rifles against men speaking the same mother tongue. Some few, however, secured the rare privilege of acting simply as despatch riders, or as members of the Boer ambulance corps.

One of the sons of my Methodist farmer friend had been thus employed at Magersfontein, but had now seized the first opportunity of taking the oath and returning to his home. With his own lips he told me that on that fatal field he had found the body of an English officer, in whose cold hand lay an open locket, and in the locket two portraits; one the portrait of a fair English lady, and the other that of a still fairer English child. So, before the eyes of one dying on the blood-stained *veldt* did visions of home and loved ones flit. Life's last look turned thither! In war, the cost in cash is clearly the cost that is of least consequence. Who can appraise aright the price of that one locket?

Yet, appositely enough, as, that same evening, I was being driven back to town in a buggy and four, a little maiden—perchance like the maiden of the locket—wonderingly exclaimed as she watched the sun sink in radiance behind a neighbouring hill: "Why! just look! The sky is English!"

"How so?" asked her father.

"Can't you see?" said the child; "it is all red, white, and blue!" Which indeed it was!

But our title to this newly-conquered territory was by no means quite so unchallenged as such a complacent and complimentary sky might have led one to suppose. The heavens above us were for the moment English, but scarcely the earth beneath us; and certainly not the land beyond us. Great even thus far had been the price of conquest; but the full sum was not yet ready for the reckoning. No new Magersfontein awaited us, and no new Paardeberg; but the incessant risking of precious life, and much loss thereof in other fashions than those of the battlefield.

Possibly one of the most distressing cases of that kind occurred only two days after near Karee, a few miles beyond Bloemfontein. The officers of the Guards had become famous for their care of their men, and for their constant endeavour to keep them well served with supplementary supplies of food. They foraged right and left, and bargained with the farmers for all available milk and butter and cheese and bread. Men on the march cannot always live on rations only, and good leadership looks after the larder as well as after the lives of the men. On this gracious errand there rode forth from the camp as fine a group of regimental officers as could possibly be found; to wit, the colonel of the Grenadiers, his adjutant and transport officer who, beyond most, were choice young men and goodly; also the colonel of one of the Coldstream battalions, and one orderly. Hiding near a neighbouring *kopje* was a small body of Zarps watching for a chance of sniping or capturing a seceding Boer. Of them our officers caught sight, and with characteristic British pluck sought to capture them. But on the *kopje* the Boers found effectual cover, plied their rifles vigorously and presently captured all their would-be captors. As at Belmont, and on the same day of the month, the colonel of the Grenadiers was wounded in two places; the transport officer, the son of one of our well-known generals, lost his right arm; the adjutant, a younger brother of a noted earl, was shot through the heart, and the life of the other colonel was for a while despaired of. It was in some senses the saddest disaster that had yet befallen the Guards' Brigade; and it was the outcome not of some decisive battle, but of a kindly quest for milk.

CHAPTER 2

A Long Halt at Bloemfontein

Before we could resume our march every commissariat store needed to be replenished, and every man required a new outfit from top to toe. If the march of the infantry had been much further prolonged we should have degenerated into a literally bootless expedition, for some of the men reached Bloemfontein with bare if not actually bleeding feet, while their nether garments were in a condition that beggared and baffled all description. Once smart Guardsmen had patched their trousers with odd bits of sacking, and in one case the words Lime Juice Cordial were still plainly visible on the sacking. So came that *cordial* and its victorious wearer into the vanquished capital. Others despairingly gave up all further attempts at patching, having repeatedly proved, as the Scriptures say, that the rent is thereby made worse. So they were perforce content to go about in such a condition of deplorable dilapidation as anywhere else would inevitably result in their being *run in* for flagrant disregard of public decorum.

The Canadians took rank from the first as among the very finest troops in all the field, and adopted as their own the following singular marching song:

We will follow Roberts,
Follow, follow, follow;
Anywhere, everywhere,
We will follow him!

Brave fellows that they were, they meant it absolutely, utterly, even unto death. But thus without boots and other yet more essential belongings, how could they?

The cavalry was in equally serious plight. It is said that Sir George White took with him into Ladysmith over 10,000 mules and horses, but brought away at the close of the siege less than 1100. Many of the rest had meanwhile been transformed into beefsteak and sausages. We also, during the month that brought us to Bloemfontein had used up a similar number. A cavalryman told me that out of 540 horses belonging to his regiment only 50 were left; and in that case the sausage-making machine was in no degree responsible for the diminished numbers. Yet a cavalryman without a horse is as helpless as a cripple without a crutch. It was therefore quite clear that most of our cavalry regiments would have to remain rooted to the spot till their remounts arrived.

Not until May 1st was another forward move found possible; and during one of those weeks of waiting there happened the Sanna's Post disaster, a grievous surrender of some of our men at Reddersburg, a serious little fight at Karee, and a satisfactory skirmish at Boshof, which made an end of General de Villebois-Mareuil and his commando of foreign supporters of the Boers; but in none of these affairs were the Guards involved.

Meanwhile the men during their few leisure hours found it no easy matter to amuse themselves. In the rush for Bloemfontein, footballs and cricket bats were all left behind. There were no canteens and no open-air concerts. The only pets the men had left were pet animals, and of them they made the most. The Welsh, of course, had their goat to go before them, and were prouder of it than ever.

The Canadians at Belmont bought a chimpanzee which still grinned at them from the top of its pole in front of their lines, and with patient perseverance, still did all the mischief its limited resources would permit; whereat the men were mightily pleased. The adjoining battalion boasted of possessing a yet more charming specimen of the monkey tribe; a mite of a monkey, and for a monkey almost a beauty; but as full of mischief as his bigger brother.

Strange to tell, the Grenadiers' pet was, of all things in the world, a pet lamb; and of all persons in the world, the cook of the officers' mess was its kindly custodian.

Mary had a little lamb, says the nursery rhyme. So had we!
Its fleece was white as snow;
And everywhere that Mary went
That lamb was sure to go!

So was it with ours! Walking amid camp-kettles, and dwelling among sometimes cruelly hungry men that lamb was jokingly called our *emergency rations,* but it would have had to be a very serious emergency, indeed, to cut short that pet's career. Yet a lamb thus playing with soldiers, and marching with them from one camping ground to another, was well-nigh as odd a sight as I have ever yet seen.

During our six weeks of waiting I was for the most part the guest of the Rev. Stuart and Mrs Franklin, whose kindness to me was great with an exceeding greatness. Ever to be remembered also was the hospitality of the senior steward of the Wesleyan Church, who happened, like myself, to be a Cornishman; and from whose table there smiled upon me quite familiarly a bowl of real Cornish cream. Whole volumes would not suffice to express the emotions aroused in my Cornish breast by that sight of sights in a strange land.

Through the kindness of these true friends we were enabled to open the Wesleyan Sunday School as a Soldiers' Home where the men were welcome to sing and play, read, and write letters to their hearts' content. Here also every afternoon from 200 to 700 soldiers were supplied with an excellent cup of tea and some bread and butter for threepence each. A threepenny piece is there called a *tickey,* and till the troops arrived that was the lowest coin in use. An Orange Free Stater scorned to look at a penny; but a British soldier's pay is constructed on other lines; and what he thought of our *tickey* tea, the following unsolicited testimonial laughingly proves. It is an unfinished letter picked up in the street, and was probably dropped as the result of a specially hurried departure, when some passing officer looked in and shouted "Lights out!"

Bloemfontein
O.F.S

Dear Mother,—I can't say I care much for this place. Nothing to see but *kopjes* all round; and if you want to buy anything, by Jove, you have to pay a pretty price. For instance, cup of tea, 6d.; bottle of ginger beer, 6d.; cigarettes, 1s. a packet. But at the Soldiers' Home a cup of tea is only 3d. Thanks to those in authority, the S.H. is what I call our haven of rest. I shan't be sorry when I come home to *our own* haven of rest, as it is impossible to buy any luxuries on our little pay. Just fancy, a small tin of jam, 2s. It's simply scandalous; and the inhabitants seem to think Tommy has a mint of money.

After a while similar Homes were opened in various parts of the town; but this long pause in our progress was a veritable harvest-time for all Christian workers; and especially for those of the S.C.A., who planted two magnificent marquees in the very midst of the men, and had the supreme satisfaction of seeing them crowded night after night and almost all day long. Every Sunday morning I was privileged to conduct one of my Parade Services under their sheltering canvas; and many a time in the course of each succeeding week took part in their enthusiastic religious gatherings.

Here, as at Modder River, secular song was nowhere, while sacred song became all and in all. I am told that sometimes on the march, sometimes amid actual battle scenes, our lads caught up and encouraged themselves by chanting some more or less appropriate music-hall ditty. One battalion when sending a specially large consignment of whizzing bullets across into the Boer lines did so to the accompanying tune of

"You have to have 'em Whether you want 'em or no!"

Another fighting group, when specially hard pressed, began to sing "Let 'em all come!" But in the Bloemfontein camps I seldom heard any except songs of quite another type; and on one occasion was greatly touched by listening to a Colonial singing a sweet but unfamiliar melody about—

The pages that I love
In the Bible my mother gave to me.

Even among men on active service, many of whom are nearing mid-life, and have long been married, mother's influence is still a supremely potent thing!

Partly as the result of influences such as these, and partly as the result of prohibitory liquor laws, we became the most absolutely sober army Europe ever put into the field. Prior to our coming, no liquor might at any price be sold to a native; and there were in the whole country no beer shops, but only hotels bound to supply bed and board when required, and not liquor only, with the result that this fair land has long been almost as sober as it is sunny.

The sale of intoxicants to the troops was equally restricted, and no liquor could be obtained by them except as a special favour on special terms. Absolutely the only concert or public meeting held in Bloemfontein while the Guards were in the neighbourhood was in connection with the Army Temperance Association, Lord Roberts himself presiding; and concerning him the soldiers playfully said, "He has water on the brain."

Through all this weary time of waiting our troops were as temperate as Turks, and much more chaste; so that the soldiers' own pet laureate is reported to have declared, whether delightedly or disgustedly he alone knows, that this outing of our army in South Africa was none other than a huge Sunday School treat; so incomprehensibly proper was even the humblest private and so inconceivably unlike the Tommy Atkins described in his *Barrack-Room Ballads*, Kipling discovered in South Africa quite a new type of Tommy Atkins, and, as I think, of a pattern much more satisfactory. Nevertheless, in one small detail the laureate's simile seems gravely at fault. In the homeland no Sunday School treat was ever yet seen at which the girls did not greatly outnumber the boys; but on the African *veldt* the only girl of whom we ever seemed to gain even an occasional glimpse was—"The girl I left behind me."

During our stay in Bloemfontein a part of the Guard's Brigade was sent to protect the drift and broken railway bridge across the Modder River at The Glen; which was the first really pretty pleasure resort we had found in South Africa since Table

Mountain and Table Bay had vanished from our view. Here the Grenadier officers had requisitioned for mess purposes a little railway schoolhouse, cool and shady, in the midst of the nearest approach to a real wood in all the regions round about; and here I purposed conducting my usual Sunday parade, but with my usual Sunday ill-fortune. On arrival I found the whole division that had been encamped just beyond the river had suddenly moved further on, quite out of reach; so the service arranged for them inevitably fell through.

But on Saturday afternoon a set of ambulance wagons arrived, bringing in the first instalment of about 170 wounded men belonging to that same division. It was rumoured that the K.O.S.B.'s, in a sort of outpost affair, had landed in a Boer trap, planted of course near a convenient *kopje*; with the result that our ambulances were, as usual, speedily required. In the course of the campaign some of our troops developed a decided proficiency in finding such traps—by falling into them!

Nevertheless, two battalions of Guards remained in camp, and they, at any rate, might be confidently relied on for a parade next morning. Indeed, one of the majors in charge, a devout Christian worker, told me he had purposed to himself conduct a service for my men if I had not arrived; and for that I thanked him heartily. Moreover, the men just then were busy gathering fuel and piling it for a camp-fire concert, to commence soon after dark that evening. Clearly, then, the Guards were anchored for some time to come, though their comrades beyond the river had vanished.

I had yet to learn that the coming Sunday was All Fools' Day, and that for those who had been busy thus scheming it was fittingly so called. At the mess that very evening our usual orders informed us that the men would parade for worship at 6.45 next morning; but within a few minutes a telegram arrived requiring the Coldstream battalion and half the Grenadiers to entrain for Bloemfontein at once, thence to proceed to some unnamed destination; and every man to take with him as much ammunition as he could carry. So, instead of a big bonfire and their blankets, the men at a moment's notice had to face a long night journey in open trucks, with the inspiring prospect of a severe fight at that journey's end. Nothing daunted, every man instantly got ready to obey the call; and just before midnight forty truckloads of fighting men set out, they knew not whither, to meet they knew not what; but cheerily singing, as the train began to move, *The Anchor's Weighed*. It was indeed!

"What does it all mean?" asked one lad of another; but though vague rumours of disaster were rife,—(it proved to be the day of the Sanna's Post mishap),—nothing definite was known; and on the eve of All Fools' Day it seemed doubly wise to be wholesomely incredulous. So I retired to my shelter, made of biscuit boxes covered with a rug; and slept soundly till morning light appeared. Then the sun, which at its setting had smiled on two thousand men and their blanket shelters, at its rising looked in vain for men or blankets; all were gone, save a few Grenadiers left for outpost duty. I had come from Bloemfontein for nought. Just behind my shelter stood the pile of firewood neatly heaped in readiness for the previous night's camp fire, but never lighted; and close beside my shelter was spread on the ground fresh beef and mutton, enough to feed fifteen hundred men; but those fifteen hundred were now far away, nobody knew where; and of that fresh meat the main part was destined to speedy burial. Truly enough that Sunday was indeed All Fools' Day; though the fooling was on our part of a quite involuntary order!

Yet in face of oft recurring disappointment and disaster the favourite motto of the Orange Free State amply justified itself, and will do to the end. It says *Alles zal recht komen*; which means, being interpreted, "All will come right." While God remains upon the throne that needs must be!

Good Friday for many of us largely justified its name. It was a graciously good day. My first parade in a S.C.A. marquee was not only well attended but was also marked by much of hallowed influence. Then followed a second parade service in the Wesleyan church which was still more largely attended; and attended by men many of whose faces were delightfully familiar. It was an Aldershot parade service held in the heart of South Africa, and in what is supposed to be the hostile capital of a hostile state.

In the course of the afternoon over five hundred paid a visit to our temporary Soldiers' Home for letter writing and the purchase of such light refreshments as we found it possible to provide in that famine haunted city. The evening we gave up to Christian song in that same Soldiers' Home; and when listening to so many familiar voices singing the old familiar hymns, some of us seemed for the moment almost to forget we were not in the hallowed "Glory Room" of the Aldershot Home.

On Easter Sunday at the two parade services in the Town Church the most notable thing was the visible eagerness with which men listened to the old, old story of Eastertide, and the overwhelming heartiness with which they sang our triumphant Easter hymns. There is a capital Wesleyan choir in Bloemfontein; but they told me they might as well whistle to drown the roaring of a whirlwind as attempt "to lead" the singing of the soldiers.

At these Sunday morning parades the church was usually packed with khaki in every part. The gallery was filled to overflowing; chairs were placed in all the aisles on the ground floor; the choir squeezed themselves within the communion rail; and the choir seats were occupied by men in khaki, for the most part deplorably travel-stained and tattered. Soldiers sat on the pulpit stairs; and into the very pulpit khaki intruded, for I was there and of course in uniform. It was a most impressive sight, this coming together into the House of God of comrades in arms fresh from many a hard fought conflict and toilsome march.

At one of these services a sergeant of the 12th Lancers was present; and his was just a typical case. It was at the battle of Magersfontein we had last met. On that memorable morning he and his troop rode past me to the fight; we grasped hands, whispered one to the other "494";[1] and then parted to meet months after, unharmed amid all peril, in our Father's House in Bloemfontein. The thrill of such a meeting, which represents cases of that kind by the score, no one can fully understand till it becomes inwoven in his own experience. So we met, and remembering the way our God had led us, we sang as few men could—

1: "God be with you till we meet again."—*Sacred Songs and Solos*, No. 494

Praise ye the Lord! 'tis good to raise
Your hearts and voices in His praise!

How good, supremely good, I have no words to tell!

On that Easter afternoon there came a sudden summons to conduct another soldier's funeral. For a full hour and a half I watched and waited beyond the appointed time, while the digging of a shallow grave in difficult ground was being laboriously completed; and then in the name of Him who is the *resurrection and the life*, we laid our soldier-brother in his lowly resting place, enwrapped only in his soldier-blanket. Meanwhile, in accordance with a touching Anglican custom, there came into the cemetery a long procession of choir boys and children singing Easter hymns, joining in Easter liturgies, and then proceeding to lay on the new made graves an offering of Easter flowers.

At the Easter evening service I was surprised to see in the Wesleyan church another dense mass of khaki. Every man had been required to procure a separate personal pass in order to be present, and the evening was full of threatenings, threatenings that in due time justified themselves by a terrific thunderstorm, which resulted in nearly every tunic being drenched before it could reach its sheltering tent. Yet in spite of such forbiddings the men came in from the outlying camps, literally by hundreds, to attend that Easter evening service; and I deemed their presence there a notable tribute to the spiritual efficiency of spiritual work among our troops the wide world over.

Easter Monday, as in England so in Bloemfontein, is a Bank holiday, and usually devoted to picnicking in The Glen, till the war put its foot thereon, as well as on much else that was pleasurable. My most urgent duty that day was the conducting of another military funeral; and thereupon in the cemetery I saw a triple sight significant of much.

At the gate were some soldiers in charge of a mule wagon on which lay the body of a negro, awaiting burial. In the service of our common Queen that representative of the black-skinned race had just laid down his life. Inside the gates two graves were being dug; one by a group of Englishmen for an English comrade, and one by a group of Canadians for a comrade lent to us for kindred service by "Our Lady of the Snows." So now are lying side by side in South African soil these two typical representatives of the principal sections of the Anglo-Saxon race; their lives freely given, like that of their black brother, in the service and defence of one common heritage—that Christian empire which surely God himself has builded. Camp and cemetery alike teach one common lesson, and by the lips of the living and the dead enforce attention to the same vast victorious fact! Next day it was an Australian officer I saw laid in that same treasure-house of dead heroes. He that hath eyes to see let him see! This deplorable war, which thus brought together from afar the builders and binders of the empire, in an altogether amazing measure made them thereby of one mind and heart. It is life arising out of death; and surely every devout-minded Englishman will learn at last to say "This is the Lord's doing; and it is marvellous in our eyes!"

The first military funeral since the reoccupation of Bloemfontein by the British it fell to my lot to conduct two days after our arrival. A fine young guardsman who had taken part in each of our four famous battles, and in our recent march, just saw this goal of all our hopes and died. The fatal symptoms were evidently of a specially alarming type, for he was hastily buried with all his belongings, his slippers, his iron mug, his boots, his haversack, and the very stretcher on which he lay; then over all was poured some potent disinfectant. It was a gruesome sight! So today he lies in the self-same cemetery where rests many a British soldier who fell not far away in the fights of fifty years ago. It was British soil in those distant days, and is British soil again, but at how great cost we were now about to learn.

That guardsman was the first fruits of a vast ingathering. In the course of the next few weeks over 6000 cases of enteric sprang up in the immediate neighbourhood of that one little town; and 1300 of its victims were presently laid in that same cemetery, which now holds so much of the empire's best, and towards which so many a mother-heart turns tearfully from almost every part of the Anglo-Saxon world. It was the after-math of Paardeberg, which claimed more lives long after, than in all its hours of slowly intensifying agony! Boers and Britons, both together, there were vastly fewer who sighed their last beside the Modder River banks than the sequent fever claimed at Bloemfontein; and all through the campaign the loss of life caused by sickness has been so much larger than through wounds as to justify the soldiers' favourite dictum respecting it: "Better three hits than one enteric."

Such an epidemic, laying hold as it did in the course of a few weeks of one in five of all the troops within reach of Bloemfontein, is quite unexampled in the history of recent wars; and the Royal Army Medical Corps can scarcely be censured for being unable to adequately cope with it. They were 900 miles from their base, with only a broken railway by which to bring up supplies. The little town, already so severely commandeered by the Boers, could furnish next to nothing in the way of medical comforts or necessities. Every available bed, or blanket, or bit of sheeting, was bought up by the authorities; but if every private bedroom in the place had been ransacked, the requirements of the case even then could scarcely have been met. Possibly that ought to have been done, but all through this campaign our army rulers have been excessively tender-handed in such matters; forgetting that clemency to the vanquished is often cruelty to the victors. So in Bloemfontein healthy civilians, whether foes or friends, slept on feather beds, while suffering and delirious soldiers were stretched on an earthen floor that was sodden with almost incessant rain. Neither for that rain can the army doctors be held responsible, though it almost drove them to despair. Nor was it their fault that the Boers were allowed at this very time to capture the Bloemfontein waterworks, and shatter them. Bad water at Paardeberg caused the epidemic. Bad water at Bloemfontein brought it to a climax. In this little city of the sick the medical men had at one time a constant average of 1800 sufferers on their hands; mostly cases of enteric which, as truly as shot and shell, shows no respect of persons. Not only our fighting-men—soldiers of high degree and low degree alike—but non-combatants, chaplains, army scripture readers, war correspondents, doctors, and army nurses, it remorselessly claimed and victimised. In such a campaign the fighting line is not the chief point of peril, nor the fighting soldiers the only sufferers. Hospital work has its heroes, though not its trumpeters, and many a man of the Royal Army Medical Corps has as faithfully won his medal as any that handled rifle.

Our "*Kopje*-Book Maxims" told us that "two horses are enough to shift a camp—provided they are dead enough." Either the camp or the horses must be quickly shifted if pestilence is to be kept at bay; yet in spite of all shiftings, of all sanitary searchings and strivings, the fever refused to shift; the field hospitals were from the first hopelessly crowded out; and the city of death would quickly have become the city of despair, but for the timely arrival of sundry irregular helpers and organisations that had been lavishly equipped and sent out by private beneficence. Such was the huge Portman Hospital. In the Ramblers' Club and Grounds, the Longman Hospital was housed; and here I found Conan Doyle practising the healing art with presumably a skill rivalling that with which he penned his superb detective tales. In the forsaken barracks of the Orange Free State soldiery, the Sydney doctors established their house of healing, assisted by ambulance men and ambulance appliances unsurpassed by anything of the kind employed in any other part of Africa. Australia, like her sister colonies, sent to us her best; and bravely they bore themselves beside our best.

To relieve the pressure thus created almost every public building in the town was requisitioned for hospital purposes; schools and clubs and colleges, the nunnery, the lunatic asylum, and even the stately Parliament Hall with its marble entrance and sumptuous fittings. The presidential chair, behind the presidential desk, still retained its original place on the presidential platform; but—"how are the mighty fallen!" I saw it occupied by an obscure hospital orderly who was busy filling up a still more obscure hospital schedule. The whole floor of the building was so crowded with beds that all the senatorial chairs and desks had perforce been removed. The Orange Free State senators sitting on those aforesaid chairs had resolved in secret session, only a few eventful months before, to hurl in England's face an ulti-

Rev. T. F. Falkner, M.A. Chaplain to the First Division and to the Guards' Brigade, South African Field Force, 1899–1900

matum that made war inevitable, and brought our batteries and battalions to their very doors. But now they were fugitives every one from the city of their pride, which they had surrendered without striking a solitary blow for its defence; while the actual building in which their lunacy took final shape, and launched itself on an astonished Christendom, I beheld full to overflowing with the deadly fruit of their doing. In the very presence of the president's chair of state, here a Boer, there a Briton, it may be of New Zealand birth or Canadian born, moaned out his life, and so made his last mute protest against the outrage which rallied a whole empire in passionate self-defence.

Among the more than thousand victims the Bloemfontein fever epidemic claimed, few were more lamented than a sergeant of the 3rd Grenadier Guards, who, according to the *Household Brigade Magazine*, had a specially curious experience in the assault on Grenadier Hill at the battle of Belmont, for—

> . . . . he was hit by no less than nine separate bullets, besides having his bayonet carried away, off his rifle, by another shot, making a total of ten hits. He continued till the end of the action with his company in the front of the attack, where on inspection it was found he had only actually five wounds; but besides some damage to his clothing had both pouches hit and all his cartridges exploded. He did not go to hospital till the next day, when he felt a little bruised and stiff.

It really seemed hard to succumb to enteric after such a miraculous escape from the enemies' murderous fire.

The following letter by the Rev. T. F. Falkner refers to this period, and was sent originally to the Chaplain-General; but is here published, slightly abridged, as an excellent illustration of the spirit and work of the many chaplains of the Church of England who have taken part in this campaign:

> I was particularly anxious that you should know the luxury in which we are living in the matter of Church privileges, and the keen appreciation which our people show of that which is so freely offered. Nothing can exceed the kind-

ness of the dean and his clergy. They allow us to have the use of the cathedral on Sunday mornings at nine o'clock for a parade service for the Guards, and at 5.30 on Sunday evenings we have a special evensong for the convenience of officers and men to enable them to get back to barrack or camp in good time; in addition to this, we have permission to hold a special mission service for soldiers on Friday evenings at 6.30. There is a daily celebration as well as Morning and Evening Prayer and Litany, while on Sundays there are three celebrations of Holy Communion. These are luxuries to us wayfarers on the *veldt*. Now for the appreciation of them. On the Sunday after we came in, the cathedral choir volunteered their help at our nine o'clock (Guards') parade, and the service was home-like and hearty. The drums were there and rolled at the *Glorias*, and *God Save the Queen*, which was sung because it was a parade service. I spoke to the men on the blessings of a restful hour of worship in an English church after our journeyings, and of the mercies which had been granted to us, basing what I had to say on 'It is good for us to be here.' At the morning service at 10.30 there was a large number of the headquarter staff present, many of whom, Lord Roberts included, stayed to the celebration. . . . At 7.30, the ordinary hour for evensong, long before the service began the church was literally *packed* with officers and men, one vast mass of khaki; all available chairs and forms were got in, and officers were put up into the long chancel wherever room could be found for them. The heartiness of that service, the reverence and devoutness of the men, the uplifting of heart and voice in the familiar chants and hymns, the clear manly enunciation of the Articles of our Faith, and the ready responses, all combined to make the service a grand evidence of the religious side of our men and a striking testimony to their desire to worship their God in the beauty of holiness. Many of us will remember that Sunday night with thankfulness. Coney preached us a very excellent sermon. The few civilians who were able to get in were much struck by the evident sincerity and devout behaviour of the men who surrounded them. And yet the Boers say 'the English *must* lose because they have no God.' One of the clergy told me a day or two after we got here that he met one of our men outside the cathedral as he was walking along, and the soldier accosted him. 'Beg pardon, sir, is that an English church?' 'Yes,' said the clergyman. 'Might I go in, sir?' 'Why, of course,' was the reply, 'it is open all day.' 'Thank you, sir; I should just like to go in and say a prayer for the wife and children;' and in he went.

I felt after our first experience that it was hardly fair to oust so many of the regular worshippers from their own place of worship, and so we arranged for the extra service at 5.30. It was to be purely a soldiers' service. But a word or two about the Friday evening special Lenten service. Familiar hymns, a metrical litany, and part of the Commination Service were gladly joined in by a large number of men, the cathedral being more than half full, and the archdeacon gave us a very helpful address. After that service a good number of men stayed behind, at our invitation, to practise psalms and hymns for the soldiers' evening service on the following Sunday, a precaution which served its purpose well. At that service the church was *filled*; Lord Roberts came to it, and it was an ideal soldiers' service. Coney and I took the service, Norman Lee and Southwell read the lessons, Blackbourne was at the organ, and the dean preached. One of the staff officers said afterwards that he had never enjoyed a service so much, and I think many others had similar feelings. But the flow of khaki-clad worshippers had not ceased, for no sooner had our 5.30 service ended than men and officers began coming in for the 7.30 ordinary service, and at that the chancel and more than half the body of the church was again filled with our troops. It *was* cheering to see and comforting to share in.

The morning of this Sunday I spent at Bishop's Glen, about fourteen miles up the line, close to the bridge over the Modder River which was blown up directly we got here, where two battalions of the Guards were afterwards sent. I had to go up in great haste on the Saturday to bury the adjutant of the 3rd Grenadiers, who was killed the day before; a very sad task for me, for having been with the battalion all along, I had got to know him well and to appreciate him highly, as every one did who knew him. I got to camp about 5.30 on Saturday evening, after three and a half hours' heavy travelling along a muddy track over the *veldt*, through dongas and drifts, and we laid him to rest on a little knoll overlooking the well-wooded banks of what is *there* a pretty river, a short distance only from the broken bridge, which stood out against a background of shrubs and trees on the river side, and struck me as a fitting emblem of a strong and useful life smitten down suddenly by an unseen hand. I stayed the night at Glen, where Grenadiers and Coldstreams took care of me, and on Sunday morning at seven we had our parade service, followed by a celebration at the railway station, at which we had a nice number of communicants.

We find the hospital work here very heavy. There are no less than ten public buildings in use as hospitals in the town: in addition, of course, to our field hospitals, which are *full*. For a short time last week I was left to do all this with two chaplains besides myself. The chaplains here are splendid, so keen and self-denying, nothing seems too much trouble; all going strong and working hard. It is a pleasure to be with such men. We are all distressed at our inability to do more, and conscious of our failure to do what we would wish; but we do what we can. The S.C.A. has two tents and are working on good lines, and the men appreciate them. Lowry and I have walked the whole way so far, save that I had a lift from Jacobsdal to Klip Drift, and I am thankful to be able to say I have not been other than fit all through. All the others have had horses to ride: they are welcome to them. I am a bit proud of having had a share in that march from Klip Drift to Bloemfontein, and am thankful for the strength that was given me to do it. I am jealous for the honour of the department, and all I want at the end of the campaign is that the generals should say, the Church of England chaplains have done their duty well. One said to me the other day, 'I *should* like to be mentioned in despatches.' I replied, 'I have no such wish. To do that you must go where you have no business to be.' Our chaplains are brave men; there's not one who would flinch if told to go into the firing line; but the generals *all* say that our place is at the field hospital; moving quietly amongst the sick and wounded when they are brought in, and burying the dead when they are carried out. There's not one of our chaplains out here who has not earned, so far as I can gather, kind words from those with whom he serves, and I think you will find your selection has been more than justified.

We had an excellent meeting in connection with the A.T.A. in the Bloemfontein Town Hall last night, with Lord Roberts in the chair. He spoke admirably; and though most of the troops were out of the city the hall was full.

CHAPTER 3

Worlds Unknown

During this six weeks of tarrying at Bloemfontein I found myself able to visit a most interesting Methodist family residing some twenty miles south of the town. For my sole benefit the express to the Cape was stopped at a certain platelayer's hut, and then a walk of about a mile across the *veldt* brought me to the pleasant country house of a venerable widow lady. Her belongings had of course been freely commandeered by the Boers on the outbreak of war; nor had the sons, being burghers, though loyal-hearted Britishers, been able to elude their liability to bear arms against their own kin. The two youngest, schoolboys still, though of conscript age, had been sent down south betimes; and so were well out of harm's way, but the two elder were not suffered to thus escape. One as a despatch rider, and one as a commissariat officer, they were compelled to serve a cause that did violence to their deepest convictions. On the first appearance therefore of the British, both brothers following the bidding of strongest blood bonds, transferred their allegiance, if not their service, to the other side. Thereupon they were so incessantly threatened with a volley of avenging Boer bullets they felt compelled to take a holiday trip to the Cape. Thus was their gentle mother with war still raging round her gates bereft of the presence, protection, and sorely needed aid of all her sons.

We arranged for the holding in her home of an Easter Sunday evening service; and then returning to the railway were cheered by the speedy sight of a goods train bound for Bloemfontein. Whereupon I scrambled on to the top of a heavily loaded truck, and there, being a first-class passenger provided with a first-class ticket, travelled in first-class style, sitting awkwardly astride of nobody knows what. On the same truck rode a Colonial, an English cavalryman, and a Hindu who courteously threw over me a handsome rug when the chilly eve closed in upon us. A decidedly representative group were we atop that truck-load of miscellaneous munitions of war. And on into the darkness, and through the darkness, we thus rode till late at night we reached the lights of Bloemfontein.

On Saturday, April 22nd, the colonel of my battalion informed his quartermaster that the next day his men would leave Kaffir River, proceed to Springfield, and thence to "worlds unknown!" That is precisely where we soon found ourselves. Early on Sunday morning I said goodbye to Bloemfontein, expecting to see its face no more, for surely this must be the long looked for start towards golden Krugerland! At Kaffir River I found the Guards were some hours ahead of me, but was just in time to catch the tail of a long train of transport wagons belonging to them, so that fortunately there was no fear of my being left alone, and lost a second time upon the *veldt*. Thus commenced a long Sunday march, as we all supposed, to Springfield. Later on we learned it certainly was not Springfield we were slowly approaching; but that possibly night-fall would land us somewhere near the Waterworks recently shattered, and still held, by the Boers. Yet "not there, not there, my child," were our weary feet wending. We began to wonder whether they were wending anywhere; and to this hour nobody seems to know the name of the place where we that night rested. Perhaps it had no name! Soldiers on active service seldom walk by sight. It is theirs always "to *trust* and obey." Even regimental officers seldom know precisely where their next stopping-place will be, or what presently they will be called upon to do. They often resemble the pieces on a chess board, which cannot see the hand that moves them and cannot tell why this piece instead of that is taken. To keep our adversaries if possible in the dark, we have ourselves to dwell in darkness; but it is a source of sore distress all the same. The troops hunger for information and seldom get it; so, to supply the lack they invent it; and then scornfully laugh at their own inventings. They would sooner travel anywhere than "through worlds unknown"; and yet somehow that becomes for them the commonest of all treks!

While the afternoon was still new we heard on our near left the sound of heavy shell firing; of which, however, the men took no more notice than if they had been manoeuvring on Salisbury Plain. They marched on as stolidly and cheerily as ever, chatting and laughing as they marched. But presently there broke upon our ears the familiar sound of the pom-pom, which months ago at the Modder had so shaken everybody's nerves. Instantly there burst from the whole brigade a cry of recognition, and every man instinctively perceived that some grim business had begun. Another Sunday battle was raging just over the ridge, and the rest of that day's march had for its accompaniment the music of pom-poms, the rattle of rifle fire, and the thud of shells. But at the close of the day an officer somewhat discontentedly reported that *if* our artillery had only reached a certain place by a certain time, something splendid would have happened. Many of our rat-traps proved thus weak in the spring, and snapped too slowly, specially on Sundays. Some such disastrous *if* seemed to spring up in connection with most of our Sunday fights, though we still seem to cling fondly to the belief that for fighting the Lord's battles the Lord's day is of all days incomparably the best. It was on Sunday, December 10th, the disastrous attack on Stormberg was delivered; and on the evening of that same fatal Sunday the Highland Brigade marched out of the Modder River Camp to meet their doom on Magersfontein. Similarly on the night of Sunday, January 22nd, our men set out to win, and lose, Spion Kop. The Paardeberg calamity, the costliest of all our contests, was also a Sunday fight; and though in the face of such facts no man may dogmatise, such coincidences, all happening in the course of a few weeks, in the conduct of the same war, make one wonder whether Sunday is really a lucky day for purposes so dread, and whether the Boers are not justified in their supposed refusal to fight on Sundays excepting in self-defence. In that respect, I at any rate, am with the Boers as against the Britons.

When night at last arrived, we had neither tents nor shelters of any sort provided for us, though the cold was searching, and everything around us was wet with heavy dew. Men and officers alike spread their waterproof sheets on the bare ground, and then made the best they could of one or two blankets in which to wrap themselves. Through the kindness, however, of my quartermaster friend, since dead, I was privileged to push my head and shoulders under a transport wagon which effectually sheltered me from wind and wet; and there, in the midst of mules and men, mostly darkies, I slept the sleep of the weary.

Brief rest, however, of a more delicious kind I had already found in the course of that toilsome afternoon tramp described above. During a short halt by the way I lay upon my back watching a huge cloud of locusts flying far overhead, and thinking tenderly of those just then assembling at our Aldershot Sunday afternoon service of song, not forgetting the gentle lady who usually presides at the piano there. Then I took out my pocket Testament, and read Romans xii.: "If thine enemy hunger, feed him." But about that precise moment the adjoining *kopje*, with a shaking emphasis, said to me, *pom-pom*, and again *pom-pom*. But how to feed one's enemy while thus he speaks with defiant throat of brass, is a problem that still awaits a satisfactory solution!

In the course of the day I was greatly touched by the sight of an artillery horse that had fallen from uttermost fatigue, so that it had to be left to its fate on the pitiless *veldt*. It was now separated from its team, and all its harness had been removed; but when it found itself being deserted by its old companions in distress and strife, it cast after them a most piteous look, struggled, and struggled again to get on to its feet, and finally stood like a drunken man striving to steady himself, but absolutely unable to go a single step further. Ah, the bitterness alike for men and horses of such involuntary and irrecoverable falling out from the battle-line of life! Not actual dying, but this type of death is what some most dread!

When on Monday we resumed our march, it was still to the sound of the same iron-mouthed music; but now at last we could not only hear, but see some of the shell fire, and watch a few of the men that were taking part in the fight. Far away we noticed what looked like a line of beetles, each a good space from his fellow beetles, creeping towards the top of a ridge. These were some of our mounted men. Lower down the slope, but moving in the same direction, was a similar line of what looked like bees. These were some of our infantry, on whom the altogether invisible Boers were evidently directing their fire. As you must first catch your hare before you can cook it, so you must first sight a Boer before you can shift him; and the former task is frequently the more difficult of the two. In more senses than one short-sighted soldiers have had their day; and in all ranks those who cannot look far ahead must give place to those who can. Henceforth the most powerful field-glasses that can possibly be made, and the most perfect telescopes, must be supplied to all our officers; or on a still more disastrous scale than in this war the bees will drop their bullets among the beetles, and Britons will be killed by Britons.

Later in the day, to my sincere grief, a beautiful Boer house was set on fire by our men, after careful inquiry into the facts by the provost-marshal, because the farmer occupying it had run up the white flag over his house, and then from under that flag our scouts had been shot at. Such acts of treachery became lamentably common, and had at all cost to be restricted by the only arguments a Voortrekker seemed able to understand; but the Boers in Natal had long before this proved adepts at kindling similar bonfires, though without any such provocation, and cannot therefore pose as martyrs over the burning of their own farms, however deplorable that burning be.

At Belmont a young officer of the Guards named Blundell was killed by a shot from a wounded Boer to whom he was offering a drink of water; and about the same time another Boer hoisted a white flag, which our men naturally mistook for a signal of surrender, but on rising to receive it, received instead a murderous volley of rifle fire, as the result of which the correspondent of *The Morning Post* had his right arm hopelessly shattered.

At Talana Hill, our first battle in Natal, the beaten Boers raised a white flag on a bamboo pole, but when our gunners thereupon ceased firing, the *brother* instead of surrendering bolted! At Colenso, a company of burghers with rifles flung over their backs, and waving a white flag, approached within a short distance of the foremost British trenches, but when our troops raised their heads to welcome these surrendering foes, they were instantly stormed at by shot and shell. At length General Buller found it necessary in face of such frequent treachery, officially to warn his whole army to be on their guard against the white flag, a flag which to his personal knowledge was already through such misuse stained with the blood of two gallant British officers, besides many men.

It is said that when Sir Burne Jones' little daughter was once in such a specially angry mood as to scratch and bite and spit, her father somewhat roughly shook the child and said, "I do not see what has got into you, Millicent; the devil must teach you these things."

Whereupon, the little one indignantly flashed back this reply: "Well the devil may have taught me to scratch and bite, but the spitting is my own idea!"

With equal justice the Boers may claim that though the ordinary horrors and agonies of war are of the devil, this persistent abuse of the white flag is their own idea. Of that practice they possess among civilized nations an absolute monopoly, and the red cross flag has often fared no better at their hands.

But then it would be absurd and most unfair to blame the two Republics as a whole for this. No people on earth would approve such practices, and doubtless they were as great a pain to many an honourable Boer as they were to us. But upland farmers who have spent their lives in fighting savage beasts, and still more savage men, are slow to distinguish between lawful tricking and unlawful treachery, and are apt to account all things fair that help to win the game.

During this long trek through worlds unknown, our pet lamb, perchance taking encouragement from the example of the two chaplains, followed us all the way on foot, and became quite soldierly in its tastes and tendencies. It scorned even to look at its brother sheep on the *veldt* modestly feeding on coarse *veldt* grass; but on sardines and bacon-fat it seemed to thrive astonishingly; and both my bread and sugar it coolly commandeered. So rapid and complete is camp-life education, even when a pet lamb is the pupil!

On the morning of our fifth day in "worlds unknown" we breakfasted soon after four, by starlight; and before sunrise were again trekking hard. About ten miles brought our almost interminable string of wagons to two ugly river drifts, across which, with much toil and shouting they were at last safely dragged. Then we suddenly halted and to our amazement were ordered to return whence we came. So across those two ugly drifts the wagons were again dragged; four o'clock in the afternoon found us on the precise spot where four o'clock in the morning had watched us breakfasting; and by the afternoon of the following Sunday we were back in Bloemfontein from which on the previous Sunday we had made so bold a dash for fame and fortune. In the course of those eight excessively toilsome days the Guards had captured three wounded Boers; but what else they had accomplished no one could ever guess. Somebody said, however, that something wonderful had been done by somebody somewhere in connection with that week of wonders; which was of course consoling; but it was only long after we learned that De Wet after laying siege to Wepener for seventeen days had made a sudden rush to reach his sure retreat in the north-east corner of the Free State; that we with other columns had been sent out to intercept him; and had as by a hair's breadth just managed to miss him. Such are the fortunes and misfortunes of war. As an attacking force, De Wet in the course of the war made some bold and brilliant moves, though always on a comparatively small scale; but in the art of running away and escaping capture, no matter by whom pursued, he has given himself more practice than probably any other general that ever lived. "Oh my God make him like a wheel!" We were a lumbering wagon chasing a light-winged wheel; and the wheel was winner!

While on this long trek I lighted on a newly-arrived contingent of Canadian mounted infantry which had come to our aid from worlds unknown. They proved to be a splendid body of men, and worthy compatriots of the earlier arrived Canadians who had rendered such heroic service at Paardeberg. Their Methodist chaplain, the Rev. Mr Lane, of Nova Scotia, seemed incontestably built on the same lines; a conspicuously strong man was he, and delightfully level-headed. I therefore all the more deeply deplored the early and heavy failure of his health, as the result of the severe hardships that hang round every campaigner's path, and his consequent return, invalided home.

About this same time another equally remarkable body, the Australian Bushmen, who, like the Canadians, had come from worlds unknown, were in the far north making their way *through* worlds unknown to the relief of Mafeking. Their advance, says Conan Doyle, was one of the finest performances of the war. Assembled at their port of embarkation by long railway journeys, conveyed across thousands of miles of ocean to Cape Town, brought round another two thousand to Beira, transferred by a narrow gauge railway to Bamboo Creek, thence by a broader gauge to Marandellas, sent on in coaches for hundreds of miles to Bulawayo, again transferred by trains for another four or five hundred miles to Ootsi, and then facing a further march of a hundred miles, they reached the hamlet of Masibi Stadt within an hour of the arrival of Plumer's relieving columns; and before that week was over the whole Empire was thrilled, almost to the point of delirium, by learning that at last the long-drawn siege of Mafeking was raised; and a defence of almost unexampled heroism was thus brought to a triumphant end.

From start to finish the Bushmen were accompanied by an earnest Methodist chaplain, whom I met only in Pretoria, the Rev. James Green, who, most fortunately, throughout the whole campaign, was not laid aside for a single day by wounds or sickness; and who, after returning home with this time-expired first contingent of Australian troops, came back in March 1902 with what, we hope, the speedy ending of the war will make their last contingent.

Between Mr Green's two terms of service I was, however, ably assisted by yet another Australian Wesleyan chaplain, the Rev. R. G. Foreman, though he, like so many others, was early invalided home.

CHAPTER 4

Quick March to the Transvaal

It was with feelings of unfeigned delight that the Guards learned May Day was to witness the beginning of another great move towards Pretoria. We had entered Bloemfontein without expending upon it a single shot; we had been strangely welcomed with smiles and cheers and waving flags and lavish hospitality; but none the less that charming little capital had made us pay dearly for its conquest, and for our six weeks of so-called rest on the sodden *veldt* around it. Its traders had levied heavy toll on the soldiers' slender pay; and no fabled monster of ancient times ever claimed so sore a tribute of human lives. It was not on the *veldt* but under it that hundreds of our lads found rest; and hundreds more were soon to share their fate. The victors had become victims, and the vanquished were avenged. Seldom have troops taken possession of any city with such unmixed satisfaction, or departed from it with such unfeigned eagerness.

My quartermaster friend and myself, unable to start with the Brigade, set out a few hours later, and tarried for the night at a Hollander platelayer's hut. The man spoke little English, and we less Dutch; but he welcomed us to the hospitality of his two-roomed home with a warmth that was overwhelming. His wife, when the war began, was sent away for safety's sake; and married men thus flung back upon their bachelorhood make poor cooks and caterers unless they happen to be soldiers on the trek; but this man, in his excitement at having such guests to entertain, expectorated violently all over the floor on which presently we expected to sleep; fire was soon kindled and coffee made; the quartermaster produced some tinned meat; I produced some tinned fruit; the ganger produced some tinned biscuits—in this campaign we have been saved by tin—and so by this joint-stock arrangement there was provided a feast that hungry royalty need not have disdained. Next our entertainer undertook to amuse his guests, and did it in a fashion never to be forgotten. He produced a box fitted up as a theatre stage—all made out of his own head, he said—and mostly wooden; there were two puppets on the stage, which were made to dance most vigorously by means of cords attached secretly to the ganger's foot, whilst his hands were no less vigorously employed on the concertina which provided the accompanying dance music. This delighted old man was the oddest figure of the three, as the perspiration poured down his grimy face. To light on such a comedy when on the war path would have been enough to make Momus laugh; and when the laugh was spent we swept the floor, for reasons already hinted at, sought refuge in our blankets; and long before breakfast time next morning landed in Karee Camp.

To reach Karee we passed through The Glen lying beside the Upper Modder, where a deplorable tragedy had occurred not long before. A remarkably fine-looking sergeant of the Guards went to bathe in what he supposed were the deep waters of the Modder, and dived gleefully into deeps that alas were not deep. Striking the bottom with his head, instantly his neck was dislocated, and when I saw him a few hours after, though he was perfectly conscious and anxiously hopeful, he was paralysed from his shoulders downwards. A married man, his heart, too, was broken over such an undreamed of disaster, and in three weeks he died. The mauser is not the only reaping-machine the great harvester employs in war time. There have been over five hundred *accidental* deaths in the course of this campaign. At the Lower Modder we once arranged to hold a Sunday morning service for the swarms of native drivers in our camp, but in that case also were compelled to prove it is the unexpected that happens. One of the boys went to bathe that morning in the suddenly swollen river; he sank; and though search parties were at once sent out, the body was never recovered. So instead of a service we had this sad sensation.

About that same time, and in that same camp, one of my most intimate companions, the quartermaster of the Scots Guards, was one moment laughing and chatting with me in his tent; but the next moment, without the slightest warning, he dropped back on his couch, and that same evening was laid by his sorrowing battalion in a garden-grave. The other quartermaster, who shared with me the ganger's hospitality and laughter, when the campaign was near its close, was found lying on the floor of his tent. He had fallen when no friendly hand was near to help, and had been dead for hours when discovered. My first campaign, and last, has stored my mind with tragic memories; it has filled my heart with tendernesses unfelt before; and perchance has taught me to interpret more truly that "life of lives" foreshadowed in Isaiah's saying: "Surely He hath borne our griefs, and carried our sorrows."

When, on the 3rd of May, we started from Karee Camp the Guards' Brigade consisted, as from the outset, of the 1st and 2nd Coldstream battalions, the 3rd Grenadier Guards, and the 1st Scots Guards, all under the command of General Inigo Jones, from whom I received unfailing courtesy. With them was linked General Stephenson's Brigade, consisting of the Welsh, the Warwicks, the Essex, and the Yorks, these two Brigades forming the Eleventh Division under General Pole Carew. On our left was General Hutton with a strange medley of mounted infantry to which almost every part of the empire had contributed some of its noblest sons. On our right was General Tucker's Division, the Seventh; and beyond that again other Divisions, covering a front of about forty miles, which gradually narrowed down to twenty as we neared Kroonstad. Reserves were left at Bloemfontein under General Kelly Kenny; and Lord Methuen was on our remote left flank not far from Mafeking; while on our remote right was Rundle's Division, the Eighth. There thus set out for the conquest of the Transvaal a central force nearly 50,000 strong—the finest army by far that England had ever yet put into the field, and led by the ablest general she has produced since Wellington. Yet it perhaps would be more correct to speak of it as the first army *Greater* Britain had ever fashioned; and in my presence Lord Roberts openly gloried in being the first general the empire had entrusted with the command of a really Imperial host. In this epoch-making conflict neither the commander nor the commanded had any cause to be ashamed one of the other.

Yet from this point onward there was astonishingly little fighting. Before the campaign was over some of the guardsmen wore out several pairs of boots, but scarcely fired another bullet. The Boers were so out-manoeuvred that their mausers and machine-guns availed them little. They fought scarcely any but rear-guard actions, and their retreat was so rapid as to be almost a rout. Within about a month of leaving Bloemfontein the Guards' Brigade was in Pretoria; which, considering all they had to carry, and the constant repairing of the railway line required from day to day, would be considered good marching even if there had been no pom-poms planted to oppose progress.

When we left Karee it was confidently predicted that the Boers would make a stiff stand amid the *kopjes* which guard the prettily placed and prettily planted little town of Brandfort. So the next day and the day after we walked warily, while cannon to right of us and cannon to left of us volleyed and thundered. Little harm was however done; and as the second afternoon hastened to its sunset hour, we were gleefully informed that "the brother" had once more "staggered humanity" by a precipitate retreat from positions of apparently impregnable strength. So Brandfort passed into our hands for all that it was worth, which did not seem to be much; but what little there was, no man looted. All was bought and paid for as in Piccadilly; but at more than Piccadilly prices. Whatever else however could be purchased, no liquor was on sale; no intemperance was seen; no molestation of woman or child took place. So was it with rare exceptions from the very first; so was it with very rare exceptions to the very last.

In this respect my assistant-chaplain, the Rev. W. Burgess, assures me that his experience tallies with mine, and he told me this tale as illustrative of it. At Hoekfontein he called at a farmhouse close to our camp, and in it he found an old woman of seventy and her husband, of whom she spoke as nearly ninety.

"Do you believe in God?" she asked the chaplain, and added, "so do I, but I believe in hell as well; and would fling De Wet into it if I could." Then she proceeded to explain that her first husband was killed in the last war; that of her three sons commandeered in this war one was already slain, and that when the other two returned from the fighting line De Wet at once sent to fetch them back. "But look at the broken panel of that door," said the old lady. "Your men did that when I would not answer to their knocks, and they stole my fowls."

"Very well," replied Burgess, "where yonder red flag is flying you will find General Ian Hamilton; go and tell him your story."

As the result, a staff officer sent to inspect the premises asked the Dutch dame whether food or money should be given her by way of compensation, and whether £15 would fully cover all her loss? She seemed overwhelmingly pleased at such an offer in payment for a broken panel and a few fowls.

"Very good," added the staff officer. "Tomorrow I will send you £20, but," quoth he to Burgess, "we'll make the scouts that broke the panel pay the twenty!"

In spite of all the real and the imaginary horrors recorded in *War Against War*, this has been the most humanely conducted struggle the world has ever seen; but would to God it were well over.

In the yard of the little town jail I saw nine prisoners of war, only two of whom were genuine Boers. Some were Scotch, some were English, some were Hollanders; and one a fiery Irishman, who expressed so fervent a wish to be free, to revel in further fightings against us, that it was deemed desirable to adorn his wrists with a pair of handcuffs. In one of the cells, it was clear some of our British soldiers had at an earlier date been incarcerated, and were fairly well satisfied with the treatment meted out to them. Written on the wall I found this interesting legend: *No.*

28696, I. M'Donald, 4th Reg. M. Inf., Warwick's Camp; taken pris-
oner 7-3-1900; arrived here 11-3-1900. Also this, by a would-be
poet called Wynn, a scout belonging to Roberts' Horse:

> *To all who may read:*
> *I have been well treated*
> *By all who have had me in charge*
> *Since I've been a prisoner here.*

The poetry is not much; but the peace of mind which could
pencil such lines in prison is a great deal!

The two best buildings in Brandfort appeared to be the
church and manse belonging to the Dutch Reformed Community. The church seats 600, though the town contains only
300 whites. But then the worshippers come from near and far.
Hence I found here, as at Bloemfontein that the farmers have
their *church houses*—whole rows of them in the latter town—
where with their families they reside from Saturday to Monday,
especially on festival occasions, that they may be present at all
the services of the Sabbath and the sanctuary. A typical Dutchman is nothing if he is not devout; though unfortunately his
devoutness does not prevent his being exceeding "slim," which
seems to some the crown of all excellencies.

The young and intelligent pastor of this important country
congregation on whom I called, was evidently an ardent patriot,
like almost all his cloth. He had unfortunately firmly persuaded
himself that the British fist had been thrust menacingly near the
Orange Free State nose; and that therefore the owner of that
aforesaid nose was perfectly justified in being the first to strike
a deadly blow. He told me he had been for a month at Magersfontein, and that he was out on the Brandfort hills the day before I called watching our troops fighting their way towards the
town. I understood him to say he had been shooting buck. What
kind of buck is quite another question. Whether as a pastor his
patriotism had confined itself to the use of Bunyan's favourite
weapon, "all-prayer," on our approach; or whether as a burgher
he had deemed it a part of his duty to employ smokeless powder to emphasise his patriotism, I was too polite to ask. But he
pointed out to me on his veranda two old and useless sporting

guns, which the day before he had handed to some of our officers, by whom they had been snapped in two and left lying on the floor. There they were pointed out to me by their late owner as part of the ravages of war. They were the only weapons he had in the house, he said, when he surrendered them.

It was a very common trick on the part of surrendered burghers who took the oath of neutrality and gave up their arms, to hand in weapons that were thus worthless and to hide for future use what were of any value. We did not even attempt to take possession of any such a burgher's horse. We found him a soldier, and when he surrendered we left him a soldier, well horsed, well armed, and often deadlier as a pretended friend than as a professed foe. Because of that exquisite folly, which we misnamed "clemency," we have had to traverse the whole ground twice over, and found a guerrilla war treading close on the heels of the great war.

This young predikant with more of prudence, and perchance more of honour, recollected next morning that though, as he had truly said, he had no more weapons in the house, he had a beautiful mauser carbine hidden in his garden. There it got on his nerves and perhaps on his conscience; so calling in a passing officer of the Grenadier Guards he requested him to take possession of it, together with a hundred rounds of ammunition belonging to it. When with a sad smile he pointed out to me the *ravages of war* on his veranda floor my politeness again came to the rescue, and I said nothing about that lovely little mauser of his, which an hour before I had been curiously examining at our mess breakfast table. Too much frankness on that point would perhaps have spoiled our pleasant chat.

In the course of that chat he candidly confessed himself to be thoroughly anti-British; and for his candour this young predikant is to be honoured; but some few of his ministerial brethren proved near akin to the ever-famous Vicar of Bray, whom an ancient song represents as saying:

That this is law I will maintain
Unto my dying day, Sir;
That whatsoever king may reign,
I'll be Vicar of Bray, Sir.

So were there Dutch predikants who were decidedly anti-British while the British were over the hills and far away; but who fell in love with the Union Jack the moment it arrived; even if they did not set it fluttering from their own chimney-top. One such our chaplain with the Australian Bushmen met at Zeerust. When the Bushmen arrived this predikant was one of the first to welcome them, and helped to hoist the British flag. Then the Roineks, that is the "red neck" English, retired for a while, and De La Rey arrived; whereupon the resident Bo-ers went wild with joy, and whistled and shouted one of their favourite songs, *Vat Jougoed Entrek*, which means *pack your traps and trek*. That was a broad hint to all pro-Britishers. So this in-teresting predikant hauled down the Union Jack, which his sons instantly tore to tatters, ran up the Boer flag, and drove De La Rey hither and thither in his own private carriage. Though to our Australian chaplain he expressed, still later on, his deep re-gret that "the Hollanders had forced the President into making war on England," when Lord Methuen, in the strange whirligig of war, next drove out De La Rey from this same Zeerust, our versatile predikant's turn soon came to *pack his traps and trek*. Even in South Africa "Ye cannot serve two masters."

After one day's rest at Brandfort the Guards resumed their march, and aided by some fighting, in which the Australians took a conspicuous part, we reached the Vet River, and encamped near its southern banks for the night. Here the newly-appointed Wesleyan Welsh chaplain, Rev. Frank Edwards, overtook me; and until it could be decided where he was to go or what he was to do, he was invited to become my brother-guest at the Grenadiers' mess.

The next day being Sunday Mr Edwards had a speedy op-portunity of learning how little the best intentioned chaplain can accomplish when at the front in actual war time. It was the sixth Sunday in succession I was doomed to spend, not in doing the work of a preacher but of a pedestrian. All other chaplains were often in the same sad but inevitable plight; and though Mr Edwards had come from far of set purpose to preach Christ in the Welsh tongue to Welshmen, had all the camp been Welsh he would that day have found himself absolutely helpless. We were all on the march; and the only type of Christian work then attemptable takes the form of a brief greeting in the name of Christ to the men who tramp beside us, though they are often too tired even to talk, and we are compelled to trudge on in stolid silence.

The drift we had to cross that Sunday at the Vet was by far the worst we had yet reached in South Africa, and till all the wagons were safely over, the whole column was compelled to linger hard by. I therefore took advantage of that long pause to hurry on to Smaldeel Junction, where the headquarter staff was staying for the day. Here I was privileged to introduce Mr Edwards to the Field-Marshal, and was so fortunate as to secure his immediate appointment as Wesleyan chaplain to the whole of General Tucker's Division, with special attachment to the South Wales Borderers. This important and appropriate task successfully accomplished, I retired to rest under the broken fans of a shattered windmill.

Mr Edwards' association with the Guards' Brigade was thus of very short duration; but some interesting glimpses of his after work are given, from his own pen, in "From Aldershot to Pretoria." I must, therefore, only add that he was early struck by a small fragment of a shell, and was at the same time fever-stricken, so that for ten weeks he remained on the sick list. Still more unluckily he had only just resumed work, when there developed a further attack of dysentery, fever and jaundice, which ended in his being invalided home. Thus, like many another chaplain, he found his South African career became one of suffering rather than of service.

CHAPTER 5

To the Valsch River and the Vaal

After resting for two days at Smaldeel, the Guards set out for Kroonstad on the Valsch or False River, so called because in some parts it so frequently changes its channel that after a heavy freshet one can seldom be quite sure where to find it. This march of sixty-five miles was covered in three days and a half; Smaldeel seeing the last of us on Wednesday and Kroonstad seeing the first of us about noon on Saturday. In the course of this notable march we saw, or rather heard, two artillery duels; the Boers half-heartedly opposing our passage, first at the Vet River just before we reached Smaldeel, and then at the Sand River, long since made famous by the Convention bearing that name.

Though Great Britain is supposed to suffer from insatiable land hunger it is a notable truth that she has voluntarily surrendered more overseas territory than some important kingdoms ever possessed; but not one of these many surrenders proved half so disastrous to all concerned as that on which the Sand River Convention set its seal in 1852. At that time our colonial possessions were accounted by many overtaxed statesmen to be all plague and no profit, involving the motherland in incessant native wars out of which she won for herself neither credit nor cash. That had proved specially true in South Africa. When, therefore, the Crimean war hove in sight with its manifold risks and its drain on our national resources, it was resolved to lessen our liabilities in that then unattractive quarter of the globe. The Transvaal was at that time a barren land, given over to wild beasts, and to Boers who seemed equally uncontrollable.

An Ishmael life was theirs, their hand against every man's and every man's hand against them. Every little township was a law unto itself and almost every homestead; so the British Government threw up the thankless task of governing the ungovernable, as soon as a life and death struggle with Russia appeared inevitable. The Sand River Convention gave to the Transvaal absolute independence save only in what related to the treatment of the natives. There was to be no slavery in the Transvaal; but no Convention ever yet framed could apparently bind a Boer when his financial interests bade him break it. So set he his face to evade the conditions both of the Pretoria and the London Conventions of later date; and the one requirement of this first Convention he set at nought. During several following years he still hunted for slaves whom he took captive in native wars; *sjamboked* them into serving him without pay; bought them, sold them, but never called them slaves. They were *apprentices*, which was a fine word for a foul thing. So was the Convention kept in the letter of it and broken in the spirit of it. For five-and-twenty years of widening and deepening anarchy that Convention remained in force, the Transvaal fighting with the Orange Free State, and Boer bidding defiance to Boer with bullets for his arguments. When little Lydenberg claimed the right to set up as an independent republic, Kruger himself reasoned with it at the muzzle of his rifle, as we have since been compelled to reason with him. So at last Shepstone appeared upon the scene to evolve order out of chaos; and though he knew it not, he was the true herald of the Guards' Brigade, and sundry others, that after many days crossed the Sand River to make an end for ever of all that the Sand River Convention involved.

The year following that in which the Convention was signed, another step was taken in the same direction and independence was forced on the Orange Free State. The people protested, and pleaded for permission to still live under the protection of the British flag; but their prayers were as unavailing as the groans of the Britons, which, as recorded in the early pages of our own island story, followed the retiring swords of Rome. Now, after nearly forty years of uttermost neighbourliness, the Orange

BROKEN BRIDGE AT MODDER RIVER

Free State, with machine gun and mauser hurls back the gift once so reluctantly accepted, and forces us to recall what now they still more reluctantly surrender. How bewildering are the ways of Fate!

The crossing of the drifts at the two rivers was almost as difficult a task as the overtaking of our ever retreating foes. The railway bridges over both these streams had been blown up by dynamite: some of the stone piers were shattered, and some of the iron girders hurled all atwist into the watery depths beneath; here and there culverts had similarly been destroyed, and at many a point the very rails had been torn by explosives till they looked like a pair of upturned arms imploring help from heaven. We noticed, however, when we got into the Transvaal that the Transvaalers took pity on their own portion of the line, and studiously refrained from shattering it. Some of them were probably shareholders. The less serious damages the Railway Pioneers and the Royal Engineers repaired with a speed that amazed us; and our supply trains never seemed to linger long in the rear of us, except when a massive river bridge was broken. Then a deviation line and a low level trestle bridge had to be constructed. At that fatigue work I have seen whole companies of once smart-looking Guardsmen toiling with spade and pick like *Kaffirs*, whilst some of their aristocratic officers, bearing lordly titles, played the part of gangers over these soldier-navvies. It was a new version and a more useful one of Ruskin and his collegiate road-makers.

Bridge or no bridge, many a mile of transport wagons, of ammunition carts, of provision carts, with sundry naval guns, each drawn by a team of thirty-two oxen, had somehow to be got down the dangerous slope on one side of the drift, then across the stream, and up the still more difficult slope on the other side. It was a herculean task at which men and mules and horses toiled on far into the night. Meanwhile, when the troops reached their camping ground some miles beyond the river, they found they would have to wait for hours before they could get a scrap of beef or biscuit, and that it would probably be still longer before their overcoats or blankets arrived. For the hungry and shivering men this seemed an almost interminable interval, and for their officers it was scarcely less trying. A devoted Methodist non-commissioned officer perceiving my sorry plight most seasonably procured for me the loan of a capital military greatcoat. I also fortunately found a warm anthill, which the Boers earlier in the day had hollowed out and turned into an excellent stove or cooking-place. I stirred up the hot ashes inside with my walking-stick, but could find no trace of actual fire, so lay down beside the mound for the sake of its gentle warmth and instantly fell fast asleep. In my sleep I must have leaned hard against the anthill, for presently a burning sensation at my back awoke me, to discover that already a big hole had been charred in the coat I wore; and alas! it was borrowed. Boer rifle fire never harmed a hair of my head, but this Boer fire did mischief nobody bargained for. Clearly our pursuit was much too hot for my personal comfort!

A little earlier in the evening another glowing anthill had been found by one of our officers, and the thought of possible soup at once suggested itself. A three-legged crock was borrowed from a native and a fire of green mimosa shrub was laboriously coaxed into vigour by a young aspirant to a seat in the House of Lords. Into the crockful of water one of us cast a few meat lozenges reserved for just such a day of dire need; another found in his haversack a further slender store, which instantly shared the same fate. Somebody else cast into the pot the contents of a tiny tin of condensed beef tea; and with sundry other contributions of the same kind there was presently produced a delightful cup of soup for all concerned. To mend matters still further and to improve the no longer shining hours, an officer caught sight of a stray pig upon the *veldt* and shot it, just as though it had been a sniping "brother." A short time after a portion of that porker took its place among the lozenges and condensed beef tea in that simmering crock. So in an hour or two there followed another cup of glorious broth, with a dainty morsel of boiled pork for those who desired it—"Oh ye gods, what a glorious feast!"

Soon after, our Cape cart with its load of iron mugs and tinned

The Deviation Bridge at Modder River

provisions reached that same crock side; while wagon loads of blankets, beef and biscuits, made possible a satisfactory night's rest, even on the frosty *veldt*, for all our well-wearied men.

Kroonstad, the but recently proclaimed second capital of the Orange Free State, is a very inferior edition of Bloemfontein. There is not a single stately building, public or private, in the whole place—the Dutch Reformed Church, afterwards taken for hospital purposes, being the best, as it is meet and right God's House should always be.

It was while I was visiting the sick and suffering laid, of course without beds, on the bare floor of this extemporised House of Healing that our ever busy commander-in-chief called on a similar errand of pitying kindliness. Fortunately for all concerned the master-mind of the whole campaign is of a devout as well as kindly type. Lord Roberts not only encouraged to the uttermost all army temperance work, being himself the founder of the A.T.A., but like Lord Methuen took a lively interest in the spiritual welfare of the troops. Yet never was a general more loved by his men, or more implicitly trusted. They reposed so much the calmer confidence in his generalship because of their instinctive belief in his goodness, and as an illustration of that belief the following testimony sent by a certain bombardier appeared in a recent report of Miss Hanson's Aldershot Soldiers' Home:

> Lord Roberts! Well, he's just *a father*. Often goes round hospital in Bloemfontein, and it's 'Well, my lad, how are you today? Anything I can do for you? Anything you want?' and never forgets to *see* the man has what he asks for. Goes to the hospital train—'Are you comfortable? Are you *sure* you're comfortable?' Then it's 'Buck up! Buck up!' to those who need it. But when he sees a man dying, it's 'Can I pray with you, my lad?' I've seen him many a time praying, with not a dry eye near,—tears in his eyes and ours. It don't matter if there is a clergyman or anyone else present, if he sees a man very ill he will pray with him. He *is* a lord!

Whether in this story there is any slight touch of soldierly imaginativeness, I cannot tell, but happy is the general about whom his men write in such a fashion; and happy is the army controlled by such a head!

On the Friday evening, a few hours before our arrival, President Steyn stood in the drift of the Kroonstad stream, *sjambok* in hand, seeking to drive back the fleeing Boers to their new-made and now deserted trenches; but the President's *sjambok* proved as unavailing as Mrs Partington's heroic broom. The Boer retreat had grown into a rout; and the President's own retirement that night was characterised by more of despatch than dignity. He is reported to have said, "Better a Free State ruined than no Free State at all." For its loss of freedom, and for its further ruin, no living man is so responsible as he. But for his sympathy and support the Boers would have made less haste in the penning of their ultimatum, and war might still have slept. *Steyn's ambition awoke it!*

Whilst its President-protector fled, Kroonstad that night found itself face to face with pandemonium let loose. The great railway bridge over the Valsch was blown up with a terrific crash. The new goods station belonging to the railway, recently built at a cost of £5000, and filled with valuable stores, including food stuffs, was drenched with paraffin by the Boer Irish Brigade, and given to the flames; while five hundred sacks of Indian corn piled outside shared the same fate. No wonder that, as at Bloemfontein, the arrival of the Guards' Brigade was welcomed with ringing cheers, and the frantic waving by many a hand of tiny Union Jacks. Our coming was to them the end of anarchy.

It is however worthy of note that the Boers who thus gave foodstuffs to the flames, and strove continually to tear up the rails along which food supplies arrived, yet left their wives and children for us to feed. About that they had no compunctions and no fear, in spite of the fabled horrors ascribed to British troops. They knew full well that even if those troops were half starved, these non-combatants would not be suffered to lack any good thing. Even President Kruger, though careful to carry all his wealth away, commended his wife to our tender keeping. Some of us would rather he had taken the wife and left the wealth; but concerning the scrupulous courtesy shown to her, no voice of complaining has ever been heard. When we ourselves were famished we fed freely the families of the very men who set fire to our food supplies; and their children especially were as thoughtfully cared for as though they were our own. War is always an accursed thing, but even in this dread sphere the Christ-influence is not unfelt.

To my intense delight after so many Sabbath-less Sundays, I found myself privileged to conduct a well-attended parade service for the Nonconformists in the Guards' Brigade at 9 a.m., and for the men of General Stephenson's Brigade at a later hour. In the afternoon I paid a visit to the native Wesleyan church which has connected with it about twelve hundred members in and around Kroonstad. The building, which is day school, Sunday school and chapel all in one, is already of a goodly size, but it was about to be enlarged when the war began. I found a capital congregation awaiting my appearing, the women sitting on one side, the men on the other. There were three interpreters who translated what I said into *Kaffir*, Basuto and Dutch; an arrangement which gives a preacher ample time to think before he speaks; though once or twice I fear I forgot when number two had finished that number three had still to follow. I noticed when the collection was taken, there seemed almost as many coins as worshippers, and all the coins were silver, excepting only two. Yet this was a congregation of *Kaffirs*!

At night, assisted by the Canadian chaplain, I took the service in the Wesleyan English church, where the singing and the collection were both golden. So also was the text; and delightsomely appropriate withal. "The Most High ruleth the kingdom of men and giveth it to whomsoever He will." Of the sermon based upon it however it is not for me to speak. So ended my first Sunday in Kroonstad, where I was the favoured guest of Mr and Mrs Thorn, late of Bristol, and still Britishers "to the backbone the thick way through."

This memorable march from the Valsch to the Vaal was, in consequence of the transport difficulties already described, one of the hungriest in all our record. To all the other miseries of the men there was added an incessant pining for food which it was impossible for them to procure in anything like satisfying quantities, and

I have repeatedly watched them gather up from the face of the *veldt* unwholesomenesses that no man could eat; I have seen them many a time thus try with wry face to devour wild melon bitter as gall, and then fling it away in utter disgust, if not despair.

Yet at the head of the Brigade there marched a strong body of Military Police whose one business it was to see that these famished men looted nothing. When a deserted house was reached no pretence at protecting it was made. Such a house of course never contained food, and our men sought in it only what would serve for firewood, in some cases almost demolishing the place in their eagerness to secure a few small sticks, or massive beams. Nothing in that way came amiss.

But if man, woman or child were in the house a cordon of police was instantly put round the building. The longing eyes and tingling fingers passed on, and absolutely nothing was touched except on payment. Tom Hood in one of his merry poems tells of a place—

Straight down the crooked lane
And right round the square,
where the most toothsome little porkers cried—
Come eat me if you please.

That, to the famine-haunted imagination of the troops, was precisely what many a well-fed porker on the *veldt* seemed to say, but as a rule say in vain. After thousands of troops had gone by, I have with my own eyes seen that lucky porker still there, with ducks of unruffled plumage still floating on the farmhouse pond, and fat poultry quite unconscious how perilous an hour they had just passed. Yet the owner of the aforesaid pig and poultry was out on commando, his mauser charged with a messenger of death, which any moment might wing its way to any one of us. No wonder if the famished soldiers could not quite see the equity of the arrangement which left him at liberty to hunt for their lives but would not allow them to lay a finger on one of his barn-door fowls. It would be absurd to suppose that, in the face of such pressure, the vigilance of the police was never eluded; and our mounted scouts were always well away from police control. As the result their saddles became sometimes like an inverted hen-roost; heads down instead of up; but they were seldom asked in what market they had made their purchases or what price they had paid for their poultry.

It would require a clever cook to provide a man with three savoury and substantial meals out of a mugful of flour, about a pound of tough trek ox, and a pinch of tea. Yet occasionally that was all it proved possible to serve out to the men, and their ingenuity in dealing with that miserable mugful of flour often made me marvel. They reminded me not infrequently of the sons of the prophets, who, in a day of dearth went out into the fields to gather herbs and found a wild vine, and gathered thereof wild gourds and shred them into the pot and they could not eat thereof. Violent attacks of dysentery and kindred complaints only too plainly proved that occasionally in this case also, as in that ancient instance, there was apparently ample justification for the cry, "Oh thou man of God, there is death in the pot."

Nevertheless, and notwithstanding the lynx-eyed vigilance of the police, the smell from the pot was sometimes astonishingly like unto the smell of chicken-broth; which clearly shows what good cooking can accomplish even on the barren *veldt*.

This amazing ability of the Guards to face long marches with short rations was triumphantly maintained, not for a few months merely but to the very end of the campaign. In the February of 1901 it fell to the lot of the Scots Guards, for instance, to accompany General French's cavalry to the Swaziland border. They took with them no tents and the least possible amount of impedimenta of any kind. But for three weeks they had to face almost incessant rain, and as they had no shelter except a blanket full of holes, they were scarcely ever dry for half a dozen hours at a time. The streams were so swollen that they became impassable torrents, and the transport wagons were thus left far behind, with all food supplies. For eight or ten days at a stretch men and officers alike had no salt, no sugar, no tea, no coffee, no jam, no flour, bread or biscuits; no vegetables of any kind; but only one cupful of mealies or mealie meal per day, and as much fresh killed meat as their rebellious stomachs could digest without the aid of salt or mustard. Yet the only deaths were two by drowning; and at the close of the operations, on April 1st, 1901, General French addressed the 1st Brigade, Scots Guards in a farewell speech at Vryheid:

Major Cuthbert, officers, N.C.Os. and men of the Scots Guards. The operations in the Eastern Transvaal are brought to a close, and I have had the opportunity of addressing the Royal Horse and Field Artillery and Cavalry; but, although you were with me in the Western Transvaal, this is the first time I have had the pleasure of addressing you on parade. The operations from Springs to Ermelo, and from Ermelo to Piet Retief, were conducted under the most trying circumstances and severe hardships. Lying on the ground, which was under water, with no shelter, with very short rations and for sometime none at all, you had to exist on the meagre supplies of the district, which were very poor. At one time it caused me the deepest anxiety, as in consequence of the weather all communications were temporarily suspended; but the cheery manner and disposition of this splendid battalion did a great deal to disperse this anxiety. What struck me most forcibly was your extraordinary power of marching. I have frequently noticed that when the cavalry and mounted infantry were engaged (happily very slightly) in these operations, I have been surprised on looking round to see this splendid battalion close behind and extended ready to take part in the fighting, and have wondered how they got there. Another important item I wish to remark upon is the magnificent manner in which this battalion performed outpost duty and night work. On several occasions news has come to me through my Intelligence Department of a meditated attack on the camp of this column, but owing to the skilful way in which the outposts were thrown out and the vigilance of the sentries the attack was never developed.

Another thing I noticed was the highly disciplined state of the battalion. It is not always in fighting that a soldier proves his qualities. Though at the commencement of the campaign you had hard fighting and heavy losses, the past few weeks stand unsurpassed, I believe, for hardships in the history of the campaign! I thank every officer and N.C.O. for the great assistance given to me during these operations. Should your services be required elsewhere, or further hardships have to be endured, I know you will do as you have done before. I wish you all goodbye.

Among those who, like myself, on October 21st left England in the same boat as General Baden-Powell's brother, the most frequent theme of conversation was the then unknown fate of Mafeking. Its relief was the news most eagerly enquired for at St Vincent's, and we were all hugely disappointed when on reaching the Cape we learned that the interesting event had not yet come off. Some toilsome and adventurous months brought us to May 21st, our last day at Kroonstad; and it proved a superbly satisfactory send-off on our next perilous march to learn that day that the long-delayed but intensely welcome event had at last actually taken place just four days before. It filled the whole camp with pardonable pride and pleasure, though the sober-sided soldiers on the *veldt* scarcely lost their mental balance over the business as the multitudes at home, and as all the great cities of the empire seem to have done. We know it was a tiny town defended by a tiny garrison of for the most part untrained men; and therefore in itself of scant importance; but we also know that for many a critical week it had held back not a few strong commandoes in their headlong rush towards the Cape; it had for weary months illustrated on the one hand the staying power of British blood, and on the other the timidity and impotence of the Boers as an attacking force. Not a single town or stronghold to which they laid siege had they succeeded in capturing; the very last of the series was safe at last, and after all that had been said about British blunderings, this event surely called for something more than commonplace congratulations. Hereward the Wake was wont to say, "We are all gallant Englishmen; it is not courage we want: it is brains"; but at Mafeking for once brains triumphed over bullets. A new Wake had arisen in our ranks, and so Mafeking has found a permanent place among the many names of renown in the long annals of our island story.

It was an admirably fitting prelude to another historic event of that same week. On the last anniversary we shall ever keep of our venerable Queen's birthday, on May 24th, the Orange River Colony was formally annexed to the British Empire, and Victoria was proclaimed its gracious sovereign. That empire has grown into the vastest responsibility ever laid on the shoulders of any one people, and constitutes a stupendously urgent call to the pursuit and practice of righteousness on the part of the whole Anglo-Saxon race. It is a superb stewardship entrusted to us of God; and "it is required in stewards that they be found faithful."

All that week the Guards continued in hot pursuit of the Boers without so much as once catching sight of them. Repeatedly, however, we scrambled through huge patches of Indian or *Kaffir* corn, enough, so to say, to feed an army, but all left to rot and perish uncut. It was one of the few evidences which just then greeted us that war was really abroad in the land, and that they were no mere autumn manoeuvres in which we then were taking part. Some of the rightful owners of that corn were probably among our prisoners of war at St Helena, spending their mourning days in vainly wondering how long its hateful unfamiliar waves would keep them captive. Others had, perchance, themselves been garnered by the great Harvester, who ever gathers his fattest sheaves hard by the paths of war.

Occasionally we came, in the course of our march, on a recently-deserted Boer camp, with empty tins strewn all about the place and the embers of camp fires still glowing, but never so much as a penny worth of loot lying on the ground. Either they had little to leave, or else they so utilised the railway in assisting to get their belongings away that in that respect they had the laugh of us continually. This final service rendered, the Boers made haste to prevent the rail being used by us; and so far as time or timidity would permit, they blew up every bridge, every culvert, as soon as their last train had crossed it. Fortunately of the long and beautiful bridge across the Vaal we found only one broad span broken.

About nine o'clock on Sunday morning the troops reached Val Joen's Drift, the terminal station on the Orange Free State

Railway. This drift it was that President Kruger had once resolved to close against all traffic in order the more effectually to strangle British trade in the Transvaal. Another mile or two through prodigiously deep sand, brought us to the Vaal River coal mines, with their great heaps of burning cinders or other refuse, which brought vividly to many a north countryman's remembrances kindred scenes in the neighbourhood of busy Bradford and prosperous Sunderland.

Then came the great event to which the laborious travel of the last seven months had steadily led up, the crossing of the Vaal, and the planting of our victorious feet on Transvaal soil. Here we were assured the Boers would make their most determined stand; and the natural strength of the position, together with the urgent necessities of the case, made such an expectation more than merely reasonable. Yet to our delighted wonderment not a single trench, so far as we could see, had been dug, nor a solitary piece of artillery placed in position. From the top of a cinder heap a few farewell mauser bullets were fired at our scouts, and then as usual our foemen fled. Once in a Dutch deserted wayside house I picked up an "English reader," which strangely opened on Montgomery's familiar lines:

There is a land of every land the pride;
Belov'd by Heaven o'er all the world beside.
Where shall that land, that spot of earth be found?
Art thou a Man, a Patriot? Look around!
Oh thou shalt find, howe'er thy footsteps roam,
That land thy country, and that spot thy home!

Boer patriotism we had supposed to be not merely pronounced, but fiercely passionate; and "a Dutchman," said Penn, "is never so dangerous as when he is desperate"; yet when the Guards' Brigade stepped out of the newly-conquered Free State into the about to be conquered Transvaal, scarcely a solitary Dutchman appeared upon the scene to dispute our passage, or to strike one desperate blow for hearth and altar and independence. In successive batches we were peacefully hauled across the river on a pontoon ferry bridge; and as I leaped ashore it was with a glad hurrah upon my lips; a grateful hallelujah in my heart!

CHAPTER 6

About Chaplains

Whilst our narrative pauses for a while beside the Vaal which served as a boundary between the two republics, it may be well to devote one chapter to a further description of the work of the chaplains with whom in those two republics I was brought into more or less close official relationship. Concerning the chaplains of other churches whose work I witnessed, it does not behove me to speak in detail; I can but sum up my estimate of their worth by saying concerning each, what was said concerning a certain Old Testament servant of Jehovah: "He was a faithful man and feared God above many."

Of Wesleyan acting-chaplains, devoting their whole time to work among the troops, and for the most part accompanying them from place to place, there were eight; and to the labours of three of them—the Welsh, the Australian and the Canadian—reference has already been made. A fourth, the Rev. Owen Spencer Watkins, represented the Wesleyan Church in the Omdurman Campaign and was officially present at the memorial service for General Gordon; but in this campaign he was unfortunately shut up in Ladysmith, so that we never met. His story however has been separately told in *Chaplains at the Front*. There remain three whom I repeatedly saw, and who reported to me from time to time the progress of their work—*viz.* the Revs. M. F. Crewdson, T. H. Wainman, and W. C. Burgess, each of whom in few words it will now be my privilege to introduce.

Mr Crewdson, who had for some years been my colleague in England, at the commencement of the war was compelled to leave Johannesburg, and became a refugee minister at the Cape, where on my arrival he was one of the first to welcome me. Possessed of brilliant preaching abilities and uncontrollably active, a life of semi-indolence soon became to him unendurable; and presently his offer was accepted of service with the troops, but instead of being sent as he desired into the thickest of the fray, he found himself detailed for hospital and other homely duties, at De-Aar Nauwpoort and Norval's Pont. Here for over twelve months he rendered admirable, though to him monotonous, service; when, lo, suddenly the Boers doubled back upon their pursuers, and attempted not unsuccessfully though unfruitfully, a second invasion of Cape Colony. The base became the front, and this vast region of hospitals and supply depots became the scene of very active operations indeed, in which the Guards' Brigade, now recalled from Koomati Poort, took a prominent part. Mr Crewdson found himself at last not where wounds are healed merely, but where wounds are made, and for the moment, being intensely pro-British, found in that fact a kind of grim content.

Few chaplains in the course of this campaign have had so extensive an experience in hospital work as Mr Crewdson, and in the course of his correspondence he relates many pathetic incidents that came under his own personal observation. At De-Aar he found a lance-corporal with a fractured jaw and some twenty other slight or serious wounds, all caused by fragments of a single shell.

"I was one of seven," he said, "entrenched in a little *sangar* on a hill. Hundreds of Boers and Blacks came up against us. One of the seven disappeared, four others were killed; so to my one surviving comrade I said, 'Look here, corporal, we'll stick this out till one of us is wounded then the other must look after him.'"

Presently that unlucky shell made a victim of this plucky fellow; but a hero it could not make him. He was that already.

A company of the West Yorkshire Mounted Infantry only twenty strong had sustained, in storming a *kopje*, no less than ten casualties. The lieutenant, shot through the base of the skull, lay in that hospital in utterly helpless, if not hopeless, collapse; and near to him was his sergeant who, while bandaging the wounds of a comrade, was shot through the bridge of the nose, and his eye so damaged it had to be removed; whilst yet another of this group, shot through the shoulder, with characteristic cheerfulness said, "Oh, it's nothing, sir. I'll be at it again in a week."

Some of them would say that, brave fellows, if their heads were blown off—or would try to!

Writing from Colesberg at a somewhat later date Mr Crewdson informed me that going the round of hospitals, where he met representatives from Ceylon, Australia, Canada, India, New Zealand, South Africa and the United Kingdom,—had filled much of his time during the previous fortnight.

"I cannot tell the sweet brave things I have heard from tongues that had almost lost their power to speak. One was a Canadian lad, who had passed through his course as a student for the ministry, and being refused as a chaplain had volunteered as a trooper, and when the chaplain tenderly asked, 'How are you, old man?' he received in a kind of gasp this reply: 'Trusting Jesus!' Another, now nearly convalescent, said, 'I have been a Christian for twenty years, but the weeks spent in hospital have taught me more of God, and of the wonders of His grace, than years of health.' His eyes glistened and then dimmed as with faltering voice he added, 'I want to say, that it was good for me that I was afflicted.'"

In the course of these incessant hospital rounds Mr Crewdson found an Australian whose leg had been shattered by an explosive bullet and who told him this strange tale. When thus wounded he fell between two rocks and found himself unable to move, but while lying there a young well-dressed Boer discovered him, and with a perfect English accent said, "Are you much hurt, old fellow?" The Australian, suspecting treachery, turned white and trembled in spite of the stranger's kindly tone. "Oh, don't be afraid of me, you are hurt enough already. Shall I get you some water?" was the instant Boer rejoinder to the Australian's signs of suspicion. The water was soon produced; and next there came forth from the pocket of that young Boer a couple of peaches, which were offered to the sufferer, and thankfully accepted.

"You must be faint with this fierce sun beating on you," said this strange foeman; and thereupon he sat upon a rock for over an hour in such a position that his shadow sheltered the wounded man, and surely, as in Peter's story, that shadow must have had grace and healing in it. Ultimately an ambulance arrived, and this chivalrous Transvaaler crowned the helpfulness of that eventful hour by tenderly lifting the crippled Australian on to a stretcher, with an expression of hope that he would soon be well again.

At the close of this unnatural conflict it is our best consolation to be divinely assured that the brotherliness which thus presented peaches to a wounded foe will ultimately triumph over the bitterness which winged the explosive bullet that well-nigh killed him.

While it is undeniable that cases of chivalrous courtesy such as this occurred repeatedly in the course of the campaign, it is equally undeniable that the Boers sometimes deliberately set aside all the usages of civilized war. Mr Crewdson, for instance, says that after the Slingersfontein fight he met at least a dozen men who declared that the Boers drove up the hill in front of them hundreds of armed *Kaffirs*, and then themselves crept up on hands and knees under cover of this living moving wall. Such strategy is exceedingly slim; but they who make use of semi-savages must themselves for the time being be accounted near akin to them. One word from the Queen would have sufficed to let loose on the Boers the slaughterous fury of almost all native South Africa, but had that word been spoken there could have been found no forgiveness for it in this life or in the life to come. Yet Slingersfontein was not the only sad instance of this sort, for Sir Redvers Buller in his official report concerning Vaalkrantz solemnly declares that then also there were armed *Kaffirs* with the Boer forces, and that there also the Red flag was abominably abused, for he himself and his Staff saw portions of artillery conveyed by the Boers to a given position in an ambulance flying the Geneva flag. The loss of honour is ever out of all proportion to the help such treachery affords.

It was at Waterval Boven I first met my assistant-chaplain, the Rev. T. H. Wainman, and found him all that eulogising reports had proclaimed him to be. Seventeen years ago he accompanied the Bechuanaland Expedition under Sir Charles Warren, and then acquitted himself so worthily that the Wesleyan Army and Navy Committee at once turned to him in this new hour of need, resting assured that in him they had a workman that maketh not ashamed. At the time he received the cable calling him to this task he was a refugee minister from Johannesburg, residing for a while near Durban. There he left his family and at once hurried to report himself in Chieveley Camp, where a singular incident befell him.

A few hours before his arrival an official notice was issued that a Boer spy in khaki was known to be lurking in the camp, and all concerned were requested to keep a sharp look-out with a view to speedy arrest. Mr Wainman's appearance singularly tallied with the published portraiture of the aforesaid spy, and all the more because after his long journey he by no means appeared parson-like. He was just then as rough looking as any prowling Boer might be supposed to be. When, therefore, he was challenged by the sentinel as he approached the camp, and to the sentinel's surprise gave the right password, he was nevertheless told that he must consider himself a prisoner, and was accordingly marched off to the guard-room for safe keeping and further enquiry. It was a strange commencement for his new chaplaincy. More than one of our chaplains has been taken prisoner by the Boers, but he alone could claim the distinction of being made a prisoner of war, even for an hour, by his own people, till a yet more painful experience of the same type befell Mr Burgess; nor did ill-fortune fail to follow him for some time to come. He was attached to a battalion where chaplains were by no means beloved for their own sake; and though one of the most winsome of men, he was made to feel in many ways that his presence was unwelcome.

Presently, however, there came an opportunity which he so skilfully used as to become the hero of the hour, and in the end one of the most popular men in the whole Brigade. When on the trek one of the transport wagons stuck fast hopelessly in an ugly drift, and no amount of whip-leather or lung-power sufficed to move it. One wagon thus made a fixture blocks the whole cavalcade, and is, therefore, a most serious obstruction. But Mr Wainman had not become an old colonist without learning a few things characteristic of colonial life, including the handling of an ox team. He therefore volunteered to end the deadlock, and in sheer desperation the Padre's offer was, however dubiously, accepted. So off came his tunic; this small thing was straightened, that small thing cleared out of the way, then next he cleared his throat, and instead of hurling at those staggering oxen English oaths or *Kaffir* curses, spoke to them in tones soothing and familiar as their own mother tongue. Some one at last had appeared upon the scene that understood them, or that they could understand. Then followed a long pull, a strong pull, a pull altogether, and lo as by magic the impossible came to pass. The wagon was out of the drift! "Brave padre," everybody cried.

His name means *wagoner*, and a right good wagoner he that day proved to be. This skilful compliance with one of the requirements of the Mosaic laws helped him immensely in the preaching of the Gospel. He became all the more powerful as a minister because so popular as a man. In many ways his mature local knowledge enabled him to become so exceptionally useful that he received promotion from a fourth to a third class acting chaplaincy, and the very officers who at first deemed his presence an infliction combined to present him with a handsome cigarette case in token of uttermost goodwill. You can't tell what even a chaplain is capable of till you give him a chance.

When Mr Wainman first reached his appointed quarters, the wounded were being brought in by hundreds from the Colenso fight; later on he climbed to the summit of Spion Kop, the Spying Mountain, to search for the wounded, and to bury the dead that fell victims to the fatal mischance that having captured, then surrendered that ever famous hill; and at night he slept in a barn with a Catholic priest lying on one side of him and an Anglican chaplain on the other—a delightful forecasting that of the time when the leopard shall lie down with the kid, the calf and the young lion and the fatling together, and a little child shall lead them. The Christian Catholicity to which this campaign has given rise is one of its redeeming features.

While the Rev. Owen Spencer Watkins, the Wesleyan chaplain from Crete remained shut up in Ladysmith, Mr Wainman remained with the relieving force, ultimately accompanied General Buller into the Transvaal, where I frequently met him, and finally, on the approaching conclusion of the war, resumed charge, like Mr Crewdson, of his civilian church in Johannesburg. No man learns to be a soldier by merely watching the troops march past at a royal review; neither did Mr Wainman acquire his rare gifts for such rough yet heroic service while sitting in an easy chair. He endured hardness, as every man must who would serve his generation well according to the will of God.

The Rev. W. C. Burgess was a refugee minister from Lindley, in the Orange River Colony, and like Mr Wainman, was early chosen for service among the troops, joining General Gatacre's force just after the lamentable disaster at Stormberg. He was attached to the Derbys., and found among them a goodly number of godly men, as in all the battalions and batteries that constituted that unfortunate column. Some of these were Christian witnesses of long standing, including no less than five Wesleyan lay preachers, and some were newly-won converts. Hence, at the close of Mr Burgess's very first voluntary service, one khaki man said to him, "I gave my heart to the Lord last Sunday on the line of march before we met the enemy"; while many more, though not perhaps walking in the clear shining of the light of God's countenance, yet spoke freely of their religious upbringing and relationships. It was possibly one such who, at the close of a little week-night service, where nearly all the men were drenched with recent rain, suggested the singing of *Love Divine, All Loves Excelling*. The character of that man's upbringing it is not difficult to divine. Another said, "I have a wife and four children who are praying for me;" while yet another added, "For me an aged mother prays." It would be strange indeed if such confessors were not themselves praying men. They were to be found by hundreds, probably by thousands, among the troops sent to South Africa. Never was an army so prayed for since the world began; and seldom, if ever, has an army contained so many who themselves were praying men.

Nearly four months after the Stormberg tragedy, but only four days after that at Sanna's Post, Mr Burgess found himself, with three companies of the Irish Rifles and two of the Northumberland Fusiliers, cooped up on a *kopje* about three miles long not far from Reddersburg. With no water within reach, with no guns, and an almost exhausted store of rifle ammunition, this small detachment found itself indeed in evil plight when De Wet's commando of 3200 men put a girdle of rifle barrels around it, and then began a merciless cannonade with five guns. That cannonade indeed was merciless far beyond what the rules of modern war permit, for it seemed to be directed, if not mainly, certainly most effectually, on the ambulances and hospital tents, over which the Red Cross flag floated in vain. In the vivid description of the fight which Mr Burgess sent to me, he says that several of the ambulance mules were killed or badly wounded, and it was a marvel only one of the ambulance men was hit, for in one of their tents were four bullet holes, and a similar number in the Red Cross flag itself. Some of the occupants of the hospital were Boer prisoners, some were defenceless natives, so all set to work to throw up trenches for the protection of these non-combatants, and among the diggers and delvers was the Wesleyan chaplain with coat thrown off, and plying pick like one to the manner born. To that task he stuck till midnight, and oh, that I had been there to see! A chaplain thus turning himself into a navvy is probably no breach of the Geneva Convention, but all the same it is by no means an everyday occurrence; and those Boer prisoners would think none the worse of that Wesleyan predikant's prayers after watching the work, on their behalf, of that predikant's pick.

The defence of Reddersburg was one of the least heroic in the whole record of the campaign, and the troops early next morning surrendered, not to resistless skill or rifle fire on the part of the Boers, but to the cravings of overmastering thirst. A relieving force was close at hand when they ran up the horrid white flag, and had they been aware of that fact we may be sure no surrender would have taken place. It requires scant genius to be wise after the event, and still scantier courage to denounce as lacking in courage this surrender of 500 to a force six times as large. That was on April 4th, and among those taken captive by De Wet was the Wesleyan chaplain. His horse, his kit, and all his belongings at the same time changed hands, and though he was solemnly assured all would be restored to him, that promise still awaits redemption.

Mr Burgess, though stripped of all he possessed, except what he wore, received De Wet's permission to search for the wounded as well as to bury the dead; and in one of his letters to me he tells of one mortally wounded whom he thus found, and who, in reply to the query, "Do you know Jesus?" replied, "I'm trusting Jesus as my Saviour;" then recognising Mr Burgess as his chaplain, he added, "Pray for me!" so, amid onlooking stretcher-bearers and mounted Boers, the dying lad was commended to the eternal keeping of his Saviour. It is this element which has introduced itself into modern warfare which will presently make war impossible, except between wild beasts or wilder savages. Prayer on the battlefield, and the use on the same spot of explosive bullets, is too incongruous to have in it the element of perpetuity.

The number of soldiers that thus die praying, or being prayed for, may be comparatively small; but even the unsaintly soldier, when wounded, often displays a stoicism that has in it an undertone of Christian endurance. A lad of the Connaughts at Colenso, whom a bullet had horribly crippled in both legs, shouted with defiant cheerfulness to his comrades—"Bring me a tin whistle and I will play you any tune you like;" and a naval athlete at Ladysmith, when a shell carried away one of his legs and his other foot, simply sighed, "There's an end of my cricket." Pious readers would doubtless in all such cases much prefer some pious reference to Christ and His Cross in place of the tin whistle and cricket; but even here is evidence of the grit that has helped to make England great, and it by no means follows that saving grace also is not there. The most vigorous piety is not always the most vocal.

After nearly four and twenty hours of terrific pelting by shot and shell, Mr Burgess tells me our total loss was only ten killed and thirty-five wounded. Not one in ten was hit; and so again was illustrated the comparative harmlessness of either

Mauser or machine-gun fire against men fairly well sheltered. This war thus witnessed a strange anomaly. It used the deadliest of all weapons, and produced with them a percentage of deaths unexampled in its smallness.

Late on in the campaign Mr Burgess was moved, not to his own delight, from near Belfast to Germiston, but was speedily reconciled to the change by the receipt of the following letter from an officer of the Royal Berks:

Truly you are a lucky man to have left Wonderfontein on Monday; and it may be that it saved your life, for the same night we were attacked. It was a very misty night; but we all went to bed as usual, and at midnight I was awakened by heavy rifle fire. Almost immediately the bugle sounded the alarm, and everybody ran for their posts like hares. From where I was it sounded as if the Boers had really got into camp; but after two hours of very heavy firing they retired. Yesterday morning, when I went over the ground, *the first thing I saw was six or eight bullet holes through your tent*; and one end of our mess had twenty-three bullet marks in it. Nooitgedacht, Pan and Dalmanutha were all attacked the same night at exactly the same hour, causing us a few casualties at each place.

It may perchance be for our good we are sometimes sent away from places where we fain would tarry. The following typical extract is taken from Mr Burgess's Diary:

Sunday, January 20th—Rode out to Fort Dublin for church parade at 9 a.m. Held parade in town church at 11. Then rode out to surrendered burghers' laager and held service in Dutch, fully a hundred being present. Conducted service for children in town church at 3.30 p.m., and at 4.30 rode out to Hands Up Dorp; two hundred present and ten baptisms. Managed to ride back to town just in time for the evening service in the church at 6.30, which was well attended, oh, day of *rest* and gladness!

As the war was nearing its close, I sent Mr Burgess to labour along the blockhouse lines of communication, which have Bloemfontein for their centre. Here the authorities granted to him the use of a church railway van, in which he travelled almost ceaselessly between Brandfort and Norval's Pont, or beyond; and thus he too for a while became chaplain to part of the Guards' Brigade.

Chapter 7

The Helpful Work of the Officiating Clergy

In addition to the eight Acting Chaplains referred to in previous chapters, some forty-five or fifty Wesleyan ministers were appointed officiating Clergymen. These, while still discharging, so far as circumstances might permit, their ordinary civilian duties, were formally authorised to minister to the troops residing for a while in the neighbourhood of their church. Many of the local Anglican clergy were similarly employed, and supplemented the labours of the commissioned and acting Anglican chaplains sent out from England. Their local influence and local knowledge enabled them to render invaluable service, and great was their zeal in so doing. While the regular chaplains who came with the troops as a rule went with the troops, these fixtures in the great King's service were able not only to make arrangements for religious worship, but for almost every imaginable kind of ministry for the welfare of the men. They were often the Army Chaplain's right hand and in some cases his left hand too. It would be a grievous wrong, therefore to make no reference to what they attempted for God and the Empire, though it is impossible here to do more than hurriedly refer to a few typical cases that in due course were officially reported to me.

The very day the Guards landed at Cape Town I was introduced to the Rev. B. E. Elderkin, who in conjunction with the Congregationalists at Seapoint made generous provision for the social enjoyment and spiritual profiting of the troops. I was also that same day taken to the Wynberg Hospital by the Rev. R. Jenkin, who, on alternate Sundays with the Presbyterian chaplain, conducted religious services there for the convalescents, and ministered in many ways to the sick and wounded, of whom there were sometimes as many as 2000 in actual residence. Among them Mr Jenkin could not fail to discover many cases of peculiar interest; and concerning one, a private of the Essex, he has supplied the following particulars:

This lad was badly wounded in the thigh on Sunday, March 11th, somewhere not far from Paardeberg, but he seems to have got so far into the Boer lines that our own shells fell around him and our own stretcher-bearers never reached him; so he lay all night, his wound undressed, and without one drink of water. Next day a mounted Boer caught sight of him, got off his horse, gave him a drink, and then passed on. On Wednesday, in sheer desperation, he wriggled to the river to get a drink, but in his feebleness fell in; was caught by the branch of a tree, and for more hours than seem credible thus hung, half in the water, half out, before he rallied sufficient strength to crawl out and up the bank. For five days he thus remained without food, and his festering wound unbandaged. On the Friday, when Lord Roberts offered to exchange six wounded prisoners, the Boers espied at last this useful hostage, took him to their laager, put a rough bandage round his thigh, and sent him into the British camp. He was still alive, full of hope, when Wynberg Hospital was reached, and responsive to all Mr Jenkin said concerning the mercy of God in Christ; but the long delay in dealing with his case rendered an operation necessary. There was no strength left with which to rally—a sudden collapse, and he was gone to meet his God. Fifteen days after he fell he was laid to rest, with full military honours, in the Wesleyan Cemetery at Wynberg. It is well that all fatal cases are not of that fearful type!

Whilst the Guards were making their way to the Transvaal, the Rev. W. Meara, a refugee Wesleyan minister from Barberton, was doing altogether excellent work among the troops at East London; and has since gone back to Barberton as officiating clergyman to the troops there, where later on in 1902 I had the opportunity of personally noting what his zeal hath accomplished for our men.

Concerning his army work while away from Barberton, Mr Meara sent me the following satisfactory report:

During the early part of my chaplaincy there were large numbers of men in camp, and we held open-air services with blessed results. The services were largely attended and much appreciated. We then established a temporary Soldiers' Home; and after a fortnight the Scripture Reader of the Northumberland Fusiliers handed me over the responsibility, as he was proceeding with his regiment to the front. The Home was on the camp ground, and so was within easy reach of the men, who availed themselves fully of its advantages. We provided mineral waters at cost prices, and eatables, tobacco, etc., and for some weeks when there was a great rush of men in camp upwards of £120 a week was taken. We supplied ink, pens, notepaper, etc., free, and we had all kinds of papers in the Reading Room. We agreed that any profits should be sent to the Soldiers' Widows and Orphans Fund, and so before I left East London we sent the sum of £43 to Sir A. Milner for the fund above referred to. Besides the Soldiers' Home, we started a Soldiers' 'Social Evening' on Wednesdays in Wesley Hall, which was largely patronised by the men. I have found the officers without a single exception ready to further my work in every way. I had also a good deal of hospital work, which to me was full of pathetic interest. I have had the joy of harvest in some instances, for some of the men have been led to Christ. When I purposed leaving, the circuit officials generously took the Town Hall for two nights at a cost of £14 for my Farewell Service on Sunday night, and the Farewell Social on Tuesday. The hall was packed with about 1500 people on the Sunday. We had a grand number of soldiers. Then on the Tuesday in the same hall there were about 1000 people who sat down to tea, including from 400 to 500 soldiers. When tea was over I was to my surprise presented with a purse of sovereigns from the circuit, and to my still greater astonishment Col. Long of the Somerset Light Infantry came on the platform, and spoke most appreciatively of my work amongst the men, and their great regret at my departure. When he had finished he called upon Sergt.-Master-Tailor Syer to make a presentation to me on behalf of the men. It was a beautiful walking-stick with a massive silver ferrule suitably inscribed, and a very fine case of razors. Then every soldier in the hall rose to his feet and gave the departing chaplain three cheers. It was really one of the proudest moments in my life.

Of the Durban Soldiers' Reception Committee the chairman was the Rev. G. Lowe, also a Transvaal refugee Wesleyan minister; and in a letter from him now lying on my table he states that he was sometimes on the landing jetty for fifteen hours at a stretch. He adds that he was the first to begin this work of welcoming the troops on landing at Durban, and obtained the permits to take in a few friends within the barriers for the distribution of fruit, tobacco and bread to the soldiers, on the purchase of which nearly £300 was expended. Twenty-five thousand troops were thus met; over £2000 sent home to the friends of the soldiers; more than 8000 letters announcing the safe arrivals of the men were dispatched, many hundreds of them being written for the men by various members of the committee. This work was most highly appreciated by General Buller; and Colonel Riddell of the 3rd K.R. Rifles left in Mr Lowe's hands £208-18s. belonging to the men of his regiment to be sent to the soldiers' relatives. Then, only a few days before his death at Spion Kop, he wrote expressing his personal thanks for the excellent work thus done on behalf of his own and other battalions.

About the same time that the Guards reached the Vaal their comrades on the right, under General Ian Hamilton, arrived at Heilbron, and here the Rev. R. Matterson at once opened his house and his heart to welcome them. In face of the dire difficulty of dealing satisfactorily with the sick and wounded in so inaccessible a village, Mr and Mrs Matterson received into their own home two enteric patients belonging to the Ceylon Mounted Infantry, one of them being a son of the Wesleyan minister at Colombo; but here, as in so many another place, while the civilians did what they could for the soldiers, the soldiers in their turn did what they could for the civilians. At Krugersdorp, so our Welsh chaplain told me, he arranged for a crowded military concert, which cleared £35 for the destitute poor of the town, mostly Dutch. So here at Heilbron the troops, fresh from the fray, and on their way to further furious conflicts, actually provided an open-air concert for the benefit of a local church charity in the very neighbourhood, and among the very people they were in the very act of conquering. It is a topsy-turvy world that war begets: but most of all this war, in which while the *kopjes* welcomed us with lavish supplies of explosive bullets, the towns and villages welcomed us with proffered fruit and the flaunting of British flags; the troops, on the other hand, seizing every chance of entertaining friends and foes alike with instrumental music, comic, sentimental, and *patriotic* songs. Even on the warpath, tragedy and comedy seem as inseparable as the Siamese twins.

Of another important fact which grew upon us later on, we gained our first glimpse during these early days. The Boers we found were in many respects startlingly near akin to us. They sprang originally from the same liberty-loving stock as ourselves. Hosts of them spoke correct and fluent English, while not a few of them were actually of English parentage. Moreover, the Hollanders and the English have so freely intermarried in South Africa that at one time it was fondly hoped the cradle rather than the rifle would finally settle our racial controversies. They are haunted by the same insatiable earth hunger as ourselves, and hence unceasingly persisted in violating the Conventions which forbade all further extension of Transvaal territory. As a people they are more narrowly Protestant than even we have ever been. The Doppers, of whom the President was chief, are Ultra-Puritans; and they would suffer none but members of a Protestant Church to have any vote or voice in their municipal or national affairs. Jews and Roman Catholics as such were absolutely disfranchised by them; and their singing, which later on we often heard, by its droning heaviness would have delighted the hearts of those Highland crofters who, at Aldershot, said they could not away with the jingling songs of Sankey. "Gie us the Psalms of David," they cried. The Dutch Reformed Church and the Presbyterian Church of Scotland are nearer akin than cousins; and when after Magersfontein our Presbyterian chaplain crossed over into the Boer lines to seek out and bury the dead, he was heartily hailed as a *Reformed* minister, was treated with as much courtesy as though he had been one of their own predikants, and as the result was so favourably impressed that an imaginative mind might easily fancy him saying to Cronje, "Almost thou persuadest me to become a Boer!"

Of all wars, civil wars are the most inexpressibly saddening; and this terrible struggle was largely of that type. Neighbours who had known each other intimately for years, members of the same church, and even of the same family, found themselves ranged on opposite sides in this awful fray. When Boer and Briton came to blows it was a *brother-bond* that was broken, in sight of the awestruck natives. It was once again even as in the days of old when Ephraim envied Judah and Judah vexed Ephraim! Nevertheless, times without number, a concert in the midst of strife, such as that described above, sufficed to draw together all classes in friendliest possible intercourse, and seemed a tuneful prophecy of the better days that are destined yet to dawn.

We can only linger to take one more glance at this type of service by this type of worker before we proceed with our story of the Guards' advance. Winburg, like Heilbron, lay on our right flank, and was occupied by the troops about the same time as we entered Kroonstad. The Wesleyan clergyman was the only representative of the Churches left in the place; and the story of his devotion is outlined in the following memorandum to the D.A.A.G. with the official reply thereto:

Winburg
O. R. C.
Dec. 21, 1900
To Major Gough, D.A.A.G.
Kindly allow me to state a few facts in order to show the

exceptional character of my position and work, both before and since the time of my appointment.

1. Previous to the occupation of Winburg by the British troops, I was employed in attending to the sick and wounded English soldiers who were brought here as prisoners of war by the Dutch Forces.

2. During a period of at least five months—as no other chaplain or clergyman was living within a distance of about fifty miles—I was the only one available for religious services, either parade or voluntary, for hospital visitation and burial duties, which were then so urgently and frequently needed. We had six hospitals, and occasionally as many as three funerals on the same day.

3. From the date of the British occupation, May 5th, my knowledge of the country and people—acquired during twenty-five years' residence in various parts of the O. R. C.—has been at the disposal of the military authorities. I have often acted as interpreter and translator, and as such accompanied the Commandant of Winburg when, a few weeks ago, he went to meet the leader of the Boer forces near their laager in this district.

4. As almost all the English population left the town before the war, our nearly empty church was then, and still remains, available for the garrison troops. About nine-tenths of both my Sunday and week-day congregations are soldiers, for whom all the seats are free.

5. Immediately after the arrival of the British forces, our church was utilised for an entirely undenominational Soldiers' Home, and books for the emergency were supplied from my library. Colonel Napier, who was then C.O. of Winburg, expressed his appreciation of this part of our garrison work, and assisted in its development. By his direction, the Home was removed to the premises it now occupies. It consists of separate rooms for reading, writing and refreshments; also rooms and kitchen for the manageress. It is still under my superintendence.—Yours,

C. Harmon

Colonel Napier's recommendation:

To Staff Officer
Bloemfontein
I strongly recommend that the Rev. C. Harmon be retained as an acting chaplain to the troops. I can fully endorse all the reverend gentleman has stated in the above memorandum. He has been most useful to the garrison and military authorities at Winburg, and his thorough knowledge of the Dutch language makes his services among the refugees and natives indispensable.
John Scott Napier, Col.
Winburg
Jan. 3, 1901

It is a supreme satisfaction to know that our men were thus in so many ways well served by the local clergy of South Africa, to whom our warmest thanks are due.

CHAPTER 8

To the Golden City

So utter, and for the time being so ludicrously complete, was the collapse of our adversaries' defence, that on that first night within the Transvaal border we lay down to rest on the open *veldt* without any slightest shelter, but also without any slightest fear, save only the fear of catching cold; and slept as undisturbed as though we had been slumbering amid hoar-frost and heather on the famous Fox Hills near Aldershot. On that particular Sunday night our tentless camp was visited by ten or twelve degrees of frost, so that when the morning dawned my wraps were as hoary as the hair of their owner is ever likely to become.

But then as the night, so must the nightdress be; and my personal toilet was arranged in the following tasteful fashion. Every garment worn during the heat of the day was of course worn throughout the chilly night, including boots; for at that season of the year we regularly went to bed with our boots on. Indeed the often footsore men were expressly forbidden to take them off at night, lest a possible night attack should find them in that important respect unready. Over the tunic was put a sweater, and over that a greatcoat, with a hideous woollen helmet as a crown of glory for the head, and a regulation blanket wrapped round the waist and legs. Then on the least rugged bit of ground within reach a waterproof sheet was spread, and on that was planted the "bag blanket," into which I carefully crept, having first thrown over it an old mackintosh as some small protection from the heavy evening dew and the early morning frost. So whether the ground proved rough as a nutmeg-grater or ribbed like a gridiron, I soon said good-night to the blushing stars above me and to the acres of slumbering soldiers all around. After that, few of us were in fit condition to judge whether there were ten degrees of frost or twelve till five o'clock next morning, when we sat on the whitened ground to breakfast by starlight. At that unkindly hour the least acute observer of Nature's varying moods could not fail to note that a midwinter dawn five thousand feet above the sea-level can even in South Africa be bitingly severe.

After two more days of heavy marching we found abundant and beautiful spar stones springing up out of the barren *veldt*, as in my native Cornwall; and we needed no seer to assure us that the vast and invaluable mining area of Johannesburg was close at hand. Presently we passed one big set of mining machinery after another, each with its huge heap of mine refuse. If only some clotted cream had been purchasable at one of the wayside houses, or a dainty pasty had anywhere appeared in sight, I could almost have fancied myself close to Camborne.

Instead, however, of marching straight towards Johannesburg, we suddenly pounced on Elandsfontein, the most supremely important railway junction in all South Africa—its Clapham Junction—and following swiftly in the footsteps of Henry's mounted infantry took its defenders delightfully by surprise. The Gordons on our far left had about a hundred casualties, and the C.I.V.'s on our right, fighting valiantly, were also hard hit, but the Guards escaped unscathed. Shots enough, however, were fired to lead us to expect a serious fight, and to necessitate a further exhausting march of five or six miles, out and back, amid the mine heaps lying just beyond the junction. Fortunately, the fight proved no fight, but only a further flight; though the end of a specially heavy day's task brought with it, none the less, an abounding recompense. Whilst most of the Boers precipitately vanished, those unable to get away gave themselves up as prisoners of war, and thus without further effort we secured a position of vast strategic importance, including the terminus of the railway line leading to Natal; but it was also the terminus of the long line from Johannesburg and the regions beyond; so that there was now no way of escape for any of the rolling stock thereon. It might peradventure be destroyed before the troops could rescue it, but got away for the further service of the Boers it could not be. Among other acquisitions we captured at Elandsfontein a capitally equipped hospital train, hundreds of railway trucks laden more or less with valuable stores, and half a dozen locomotives with full head of steam on; so that had we arrived a little less suddenly, locomotives, trains and empty trucks would all have eluded our grasp and got safely to Pretoria. It was indeed an invaluable haul, especially for haulage purposes, and we had tramped 130 miles in the course of a single week to secure it!

Long after dark, weary and footsore and famished, we stumbled back three miles to our chosen camping ground. Since the previous evening some of the Scots Guards had managed to secure only a hasty drink of coffee, so they told me, as their sole rations for the four-and-twenty hours; but they seemed as happy as they were hungry, like men proudly conscious that they had done a good day's work that brought them, so they fondly supposed, perceptibly nearer home. Assisted by many an undesirable expletive, they staggered and darkly groped their way over some of the very roughest ground we had thus far been required to traverse; they got repeatedly entangled in a profusion of barbed wire; scrambled into deep railway ditches, then scrambled out again; till at last they reached their appointed resting-place, and in dead darkness proceeded as best they could to cook their dinners.

Greatly to our surprise the people, who seemed mostly Dutch or of Dutch relationship, received us like those in the Orange Free State towns, with demonstrative kindness; and in many a case brought out their last loaf as a most welcome gift to the just then almost ravenous soldiery. Every scrap of available provisions was eagerly bought up, and here as elsewhere honestly paid for, often at prices that seemed far from honest. Months after at this very place I learned that eggs were being sold at from ten to fifteen shillings a dozen, and fowls at seven shillings a-piece!

An Australian correspondent of the London *Times* declares that as it was with us, so was it with the troops that he accompanied. About the very time we reached this Germiston Junction, his men, he says, were practically starving; and any other army in the world would have commandeered whatever food came in its way. He was with Rundle's Brigade, "the starving Eighth" as they were well called, seeing that for a while they were rationed on one and a half biscuits a day. Yet they gave Mr Stead's "ill-treated women" two shillings a loaf for bread that sixpence would have well paid for, and no one was allowed to bring foodstuffs away from any farmhouse without getting a written receipt from the vendor. If the military police caught a ragged Leinster packing a chicken down his trouser leg through a big hole in the seat, and he could not show a receipt for the bird, away went the man's purchase to the nearest Field Hospital. To this same representative of the Press the wife of a farmer still out fighting our troops naïvely said, "For goodness sake do keep those wicked Colonials away; I am terrified of them" (he was himself a Colonial)—"but I am so glad when the English come; they pay me so well."

That was the experience of almost all who had anything to sell, alike in town and country; and this particular Frau confessed to having made a profit of ten clear pounds in a single week out of the bread sold to the British soldiers. It is said, however, that in some cases when they asked for bread our men got a bullet. Around many a farmstead there hovered far worse dangers than the danger of being fleeced.

At Elandsfontein an almost frantic welcome was awarded us by the crowds of *Kaffirs* that eagerly watched our coming. As we marched through their Location almost the only darkie I spoke to happened to be a well-dressed intelligent Wesleyan, who said to me, "Good Boss, we are truly glad that you have come; for the last seven months the Boers have made us work without any wages except the *sjambok* across our backs."

It is only fair to add that the burghers on commando during those same seven months were supposed to receive no wages; and the *Kaffirs*, who were commandeered for various kinds of service in connection with the war, could scarcely expect the Boer Government to deal more generously with them. From the very beginning, however, the *Kaffirs* in the Transvaal were often made to feel that their condition was near akin to that of slaves. The clauses in the Sand River Convention which were intended to be the Magna Carta of their liberties proved a delusion and a snare. Recent years, however, have effected immense improvements in their relative position and importance. Since the mines were opened their labour has been keenly competed for, and a more considerate feeling concerning them pervades all classes; but they are still regarded by many of their masters as having no actual rights either in Church or State. So when a victorious English army appeared upon the scene they fondly thought the day of their full emancipation had dawned, and in wildly excited accents they shouted as we passed, *"Victoria! Victoria!"* Whereupon our scarcely less excited lads in responsive shouts replied, "*Pre*toria! *Pre*toria!"

Surely never was the inner meaning and significance of a great historic event more aptly voiced. The natives beheld in the advent of English rule the promise of ampler liberty and enlightenment under Victoria the Good; but the hearts of the soldiers were set on the speedy capture of Pretoria, as the crowning outcome of all their toil, and their probable turning-point towards home. Well said both! Pretoria! Victoria!

Lord Roberts' rapid march rescued from impending destruction the costly machinery and shafting of the Witwaterrand gold mines, in which capital to the extent of many millions had been sunk, and out of which many hundreds of millions are likely to be dug. By some strange freak of nature this lofty ridge, lying about 6000 feet above the sea level, and forming a narrow gold-bearing bed over a hundred miles long, is by universal confession the richest treasure-house the ransackers of the whole earth have yet brought to light. "The wealth of Ormuz or of Ind," immortalised by Milton's most majestic epic, the wealth of the Rand completely eclipses, and nothing imagined in the glowing pages of the *Arabian Nights* rivals in solid worth the sober realities now being unearthed along this uninviting ridge. It fortunately was not in the power of the Boer Government to carry off this as yet ungarnered treasure, or it would certainly have shared the fate of the cart-loads of gold in bar and coin with which President Kruger decamped from Pretoria; but it is beyond all controversy that many of that Government's officials favoured the proposal to wreck, as far as dynamite could, both the machinery and mines in mere wanton revenge on the hated Outlanders that mainly owned them. That policy was thwarted by the swiftfootedness of the troops, and by the tactfulness of Commandant Krause, through whose arranging Johannesburg was peacefully surrendered; but who now, by some strange irony of fate, lies a felon in an English jail!

Nevertheless, later on enough mischief of this type was done to demonstrate how deadly a blow a few desperate men might have dealt at the chief industry of South Africa; and concerning it Sir Alfred Milner wrote as follows:

Fortunately the damage done to the mines has not been large relatively to the vast total amount of the fixed capital sunk in them. The mining area is excessively difficult to guard against purely predatory attacks having no military purpose, because it is, so to speak, *all length and no breadth*, one long thin line stretching across the country from east to west for many miles. Still, garrisoned as Johannesburg now is, it is only possible successfully to attack a few points in it. Of the raids hitherto made, and they have been fairly numerous, only one resulted in any serious damage. In that instance the injury done to the single mine attacked amounted to £200,000, and it is estimated that the mine is put out of working for two years. This mine is only one out of a hundred, and is not by any means one of the most important. These facts may afford some indication of the ruin which might have been inflicted, not only on the Transvaal and all South Africa, but on many European interests, if that general destruction of mine works which was contemplated just before our occupation of Johannesburg had been carried out. However serious in some respects may have been the military consequences of our rapid advance to Johannesburg, South Africa owes more than is commonly recognised to that brilliant dash put forward by which the vast mining apparatus, the foundation of all her wealth, was saved from the ruin threatening it.

That this wonderful discovery of wealth was indirectly the main cause of the war is undeniable. But for the gold the children of "Oden the Goer," whose ever restless spirit has sent them round the globe, would never have found their way in any large numbers to the Transvaal. There would have been no overmastering Outlander element, no incurable race competitions and quarrels, no unendurable wrongs to redress; the Boer Republic might again have become bankrupt, or broken up into rival chieftaincies as of old, but it could not have become a menace to Great Britain, and would never have rallied the whole Empire to repel its assault on the Empire. It is too usually with blood that gold is bought!

The war was practically the purchase price of this prodigious wealth, but it effected no transfer in the ownership. It may have in part to provide for the expenses of the war, but it is not claimed by the British Government as part of the spoils of war; and when Local Government is granted it will still be included in local assets. The capitalists, colonists and *Kaffirs* who live and thrive through the mines will thrive yet more as the result of juster laws, ample security, and a more honest administration; but the soldiers whose heroism brought to pass the change profit nothing by it. The niggers driving our carts were paid £4 a month, while the khaki men who did the actual fighting were required to content themselves with anything over about fifteen pence a day.

When Cortez, with his accompanying Spaniards, discovered Mexico, he sent word to its ruler, Montezuma, that his men were suffering from a peculiar form of heart disease which only gold could cure; so he desired him of his royal bounty to send them gold and still more gold. In the end those Spanish leeches drained the country dry; though when convoying their treasure across the sea no small portion of it was seized by English warships, and shared as loot among the captors. After the treasure ship *Hermione* had thus been secured off Cadiz by the *Actaean* and the *Favorite*, each captain received £65,000 as prize-money (so Fitchett tells us); each lieutenant, £13,000; each petty officer, £2000; and each seaman, £500. Our fighting men and officers found in the Transvaal vastly ampler wealth, but no such luck and no such loot. Well would it be, however, if these mining Directorates when about to declare their next dividends should bethink them generously of the widows and orphans of those whose valour and strong-footedness rescued their mines from imminent plunder and destruction.

Johannesburg, which we entered unopposed on May 31st, though it covers an enormous area and contains several fine buildings, is only fourteen years old, and consequently is still very largely in the corrugated iron stage of development which is always unlovely, and in this case proved specially so. Many of the houses were deserted, most of the stores were roughly barricaded, and there were signs not a few of recent violence and wholesale theft, at which none need wonder. Long before the war broke out there was presented to President Kruger and his Raad a petition for redress of grievances signed, as already stated, by adult male Outlanders that are said to have outnumbered the total Boer male population at that time of the whole Transvaal. Most of those who signed were resident on the Rand; and as soon as war hove in sight these "undesirables" were hurried across the border, leaving behind them in many cases well-furnished houses and well-stocked shops. More than ten thousand of them took up arms in defence of the Empire, and what befell their property is best told by the one Wesleyan minister who was privileged to remain all the time in the town, was the first to greet me when with the Guards I marched into the Market Square, and soon after established our first Wesleyan Soldiers' Home in the Transvaal. He, the Rev. S. L. Morris, on that point writes as follows:

President Kruger proclaimed Sunday, May 27th, and the two following days, as days of humiliation and prayer. Notices to this effect were sent to officials and ministers, and doubtless there were many who devoutly followed the directions. The conduct of one large section of the Dutch people of Johannesburg was, however, very strange. In Johannesburg, as in Pretoria, the last ten years have seen the development of special locations where the lowest class of Dutch people reside. For the most part these are the families of landless Boers. Until recent years they lived as squatters on the farms of their more thrifty compatriots. Their life then was one of progressive degradation. Under the Kruger policy hundreds of such families were encouraged to settle in the neighbourhood of the towns. Plots of ground were given them, and there they built rough shanties, and formed communities which were a South African counterpart to the submerged tenth of England. There was this difference, that these *bywoners* became a great strength to the Kruger party. The males of sixteen years of age and upwards had all the privileges which were denied to the most influential of the *Uitlanders*. It was the votes of Vrededorp, the poor Dutch quarter, that decided the representation of Johannesburg in the *Volksraad*. On the days of humiliation and prayer, when the army under Lord Roberts was within twenty miles of Johannesburg, the families of these poor burghers broke into the commissariat stores of their own Government, into the food depots from which doles had been distributed, and into private stores; taking away to their homes, goods, clothing and provisions of all sorts. Those who witnessed the invasion of the great goods sheds where the Republican commissariat had its headquarters say that the people defied the officials, daring them to shoot them. I met many of these people returning to their homes laden with spoils. Sometimes there was a wheelbarrow heaped up with sacks of flour, or tins of biscuits, or preserved meat. Men, women, children and *Kaffir* "boys" trudged along with similar articles, or with bundles of boots and clothing. Dr Krause, the commandant, did his best to secure order and to repress looting, but he lacked the reliable agents who alone could have controlled the people. This sort of thing was going on on Monday and Tuesday, May 28th and 29th. But for the astonishing marches by which Lord Roberts paralysed opposition, and which enabled him to summon the town to surrender on the Wednesday morning, it is hard to say what limit could have been put to the disorder. In all probability the dangerous section of the large Continental element in the population would have broken out into crime. Looting had hitherto been confined to the property which was left unprotected, and few unoccupied houses had not been ransacked; but had the British occupation been delayed a few days the consequences would have been disastrous.

As on that Thursday morning we tramped steadily from Germiston to Johannesburg we were greatly surprised to find near each successive mine crowds of natives all with apparently well oiled faces that literally shone in the sunlight; but natives of every conceivable shade of sableness, and in some cases of almost every permissible approach to nudity. They were for the most part what are called "raw *Kaffirs*"; and as we were astonished at their numbers after so many months of war and consequent stoppage of work, so were they also astonished at our numbers, and confided to our native minister their wonder at finding there were so many Englishmen in all the world as they that day saw upon the Rand. It was a vitally important object lesson that by this time has made its beneficent influence felt among all the tribes of the South African sub-continent.

About noon, so Mr Morris told me, a company of Lancers came into the open space in front of the Court-house, and formed a hollow square around the flagstaff. Not long after Lord Roberts with his Staff, and Commandant Krause, rode into the square; then the Vierkleur slid down the staff, and instantly after up went Lady Roberts' little silken Union Jack. The British flag floated at last over this essentially British town, the sure pledge as we hope of honest government and of equal rights alike for Briton and for Boer. It was two o'clock before the Guards' Brigade reached this saluting point, but till nearly midnight one continuous stream of men and horses, of guns and ambulances, passed through the streets to their respective camping grounds. These well fagged troops by their fitness, even more than by their numbers, astonished many an onlooker who was by no means a "raw *Kaffir*"; and one old Dutchman expressed the thought of many minds when he said, "You seem able to turn out soldiers by machinery, *all of the same age!*"

My excellent host of that red-letter day adds: "It is intensely gratifying to be able, after the lapse of more than nine months, to give our soldiers the same good name that was so well deserved then. To deny that there had been any offences would be ridiculous; but the absence of serious crime, and more particularly of gross offences, must be acknowledged to confer upon our South African army a unique distinction." That witness is true!

CHAPTER 9

Pretoria—the City of Roses

War and worship live only on barest speaking terms, and to the latter the former makes few concessions; so it came to pass that Whitsunday, like so many another Sunday spent in South Africa, found us again upon the march, with the inevitable result that no parade service could possibly be held. Everybody, however, seemed full of confident expectation that the next day we should reach Pretoria, and perhaps take possession of it. "If we take Pretoria on Whit-Monday," said one of the Guardsmen, "they will get the news in England next day, and then that will be Wet Tuesday;" which was a prophecy that seemed not in the least unlikely to be fulfilled, inasmuch as an Englishman's favourite way of showing his supreme delight is by accepting an extra drink, or offering one. Others were of opinion that, with a ring of forts around Pretoria on which hundreds of thousands of pounds had been expended, the Boer commanders would make a desperate stand in defence of their much loved capital, and so keep us at bay for many a day. But nothing daunted by such uncertainties as to what might be awaiting them, our men were on the march towards those famous forts early on Monday morning, and we soon found a lively Bank Holiday was in store for us. Shortly after noon, General French's cavalry having worked round to the north of the town, General Pole Carew prepared to attack on the south and our bombardment of the forts began, but drew from them no reply. All the Boer guns were elsewhere; and a little way behind our own busy naval guns, though hidden by the crest of the hill, lay the Grenadier Guards awaiting orders to take their place and part in the fray.

Presently a sharp succession of Boer shells, intended for the aforesaid naval guns, came flying over our heads, and dropping among our men. One hit a horse, which no man will ride again; one struck an ambulance wagon, and scared its solitary fever patient almost out of his senses; one dropped close to where a group of generals had just before met in consultation; but only one of these Boer Whitsuntide presents burst, and even that, strange to tell, caused no casualties, though it drove a few kilted heroes to run for refuge into a deepish pit, near which I sat upon the ground, and watching, wondered where the next shell would burst. When a little later the Guards moved further to the right to take up a position still nearer to the town, Boer bullets came flying over that same ridge and planted themselves among our left flank men; but when we tried to pick up some of these leaden treasures to keep as curios, so deeply imbedded were they in the soil they could not be removed. Yet they were playfully spoken of as *spent* bullets.

This grim music of gun and rifle was maintained almost till sunset, and then died away, leaving us in doubt whether the next day would witness a renewal of the fight, or whether, as on so many former occasions, the Boers under cover of the darkness would execute yet another strategic movement to the rear. That night we slept once more on the open *veldt*, made black by the vast sweep of recent grass fires; and next morning, after a starlight breakfast, I as usual retired to kneel in humble prayer, imploring the Divine guardianship and guidance for all in the midst of whom I dwelt. Presently I was startled by an outburst of wildest cheering from one group; and a moment after from a second; so springing to my feet I found our lads hurling their helmets in the air, and shouting like men demented. Not for the chaplains only that glad hour turned prayer to praise, and thrilled all hearts with patriotic if not pious pride.

An officer was riding post-haste from point to point where our men were massed, bearing the delicious tidings that Pretoria too had unconditionally surrendered. The news swiftly sped from battalion to battery, and from battery to battalion. First here, then there, then far away yonder, the cheering rang out clear and loud as a trumpet call. Comrade congratulated comrade, while Christian men, with tear-filled eyes, reverently looked up and rendered thanks to Him of whom it is written, "Thine is the victory."

Remembering how feeble Mafeking was held for months by the merest handful of men pitted against a host, it is not easy to understand why this city of roses, so pretty, and of which the Boers were all so proud, was opened to its captors after only the merest pretence at opposition. Lord Roberts is reported to have said that in his opinion it occupied the strongest position he had yet seen in all South Africa; and to my non-professional mind it instantly brought to remembrance the familiar lines which tell how round about Jerusalem the hilly bulwarks rise. The surrender of such a centre of their national life must have been to the burghers like the plucking out of a right eye, or the cutting off of a right hand. How came it to pass, without an effort to hinder it?

The German expert, Count Sternberg, who accompanied the Boers throughout the war, declared that though considered from the continental standpoint they are bad soldiers; in their own country, in ambushes or stratagems, which constitute their favourite type of warfare, "they are simply superb." He adds they would have achieved much greater success if they had not abandoned all idea of taking the offensive. "For that they lack courage; and to that lack of courage they owe their destruction."

But their flight, like their long after continuance in guerrilla types of warfare, points to quite another cause than this lack of courage. The Boer is proverbially a lover of his own; and so, though with liberal hand he laid waste bridge and culvert and plant, as he retreated along the railway line through the Orange River Colony, which was not his own, he became quite miserly in his use of dynamite when the Transvaal was reached, which was his own, and which would infallibly be restored to him, so he reckoned, when the war was over. So was it to be with Pretoria too! To the very last the fighting Boer believed that whatever his fate in the field of battle, if he were only dogged enough, and in any fashion prolonged the strife sufficiently, British patience would tire, as it had tired before; British plans and purposes and pledges would all be abandoned as aforetime they had been abandoned, and he would thus secure, even in the face of defeat, the fruits of victory. The importunate widow is the one New Testament character "the brother" implicitly believes in and imitates. Her tactics were his before the war, in the matter of the Conventions; and the wasteful prolonging of the war was a part of the same policy. Great Britain was to be forced by sheer weariness to give back to the Transvaal in some form its coveted independence, and with it, of course, Pretoria also. So he would on no account consent to let the city be bombarded. Our peaceful occupation was the best possible protection for property that would presently be again his own; and while he still went on with his desultory fighting we were quite welcome, at our own expense, to feed every Boer family we could find.

Thus, like our own hunted Pretender, he held that however long delayed, the end was bound to restore to him his own; and he had not far to look for what justified the fallacy. In 1881, for instance, as one among many illustrations, an English general at Standerton formally assured the Boers that the Vaal would flow backward through the Drakenberg Hills before the British would withdraw from the Transvaal. Three successive Secretaries of State, three successive High Commissioners, and two successive Houses of Commons deliberately endorsed that official assurance; yet though the Vaal turned not back Great Britain did; and to that magnanimous forgetting of the nation's oft-repeated pledge was due in part this new war and its intolerable prolonging. It does not pay thus to say and then unsay. Thereby all confidence, all sense of finality, is killed.

"Take your Grenadiers and open the ball," said Sir John Moore, as he appointed to his men their various positions in the famous fight at Corunna; and on this memorable 5th of June when the British finally took possession of Pretoria the Guards as at Belmont were again privileged to "open the ball." But whilst they were busy seizing the railway station and stock, with other points of strategic importance, I took my first hasty stroll through the city; and among the earliest objects of interest I came upon was the pedestal of a monument, with the scaffolding still around it, but quite complete, except that the actual statue which was to crown and constitute the summit was not there.

"Whose monument is that?" I meekly asked.

"Paul Kruger's," was the prompt reply; "but the statue, made in Rome, has not yet arrived, being detained at Delagoa Bay."

That statue now probably never will arrive, and possibly enough some other figure,—perchance that of Victoria the Good,—will ultimately be placed on that expectant pedestal, so making the monument complete. "Which thing," as St Paul would say, "is an allegory!" That monument in its present form is a precise epitome of the man it was meant to honour. It is most complete by reason of its very incompleteness. The chief feature in this essentially strong man's career, as also in his monument, has reference to the foundation work he wrought. It was the finish that was a failure, and in much more important matters than this pile of chiselled granite, the work the late President commenced in the Transvaal its new rulers must make it their business to carry on, and, in worthier fashion, complete. We cannot begin *de novo*. For better for worse, on foundations laid by Boers, Britons must be content to build.

Close by, forming the main feature on one side of the city Square, stood a remarkably fine building, intended to serve as a palace of justice, but, like the monument in front of it, it was still unfinished. In the Transvaal there was as yet no counterpart to that most important clause in our own Magna Carta, which says "We will not sell justice to any man." Corruption and coercion were familiar forces alike in the making and the administration of its laws. In more senses than one the Transvaal Government had not yet opened its courts of justice. They mutely awaited the coming of the new regime.

In one of the main streets leading out of the Square stood the President's private residence; a gift-house, so it is said, accepted by him as a recompense for favours received. Compared with the Residency at Bloemfontein it is a singularly unpretentious dwelling and was in keeping rather with the economic habits, than with the private wealth, or official status, of its chief oc-

Dopper church opposite President Kruger's house built by the late president

cupant. British sentinels had already been posted all about the place, and on the veranda sat a British officer with a long row of mausers lying at his feet. There too, one on each side of the main entrance, crouched Kruger's famous marble lions, silently watching that day's novel proceedings. Not even the presence of those men in khaki, nor that sad array of surrendered rifles, sufficed to draw from those stony guardians of their master's home so much as a muffled growl. They are believed to be of British origin, and I suspect that, so far as their nature permits, they cherish British sympathies; for they certainly showed no signs of lamenting over the ignoble departure of their lord. All regardless of the griefs of his deserted lady, they still placidly licked their paws; and as I cast on them a parting glance they gave to me, or seemed to, a knowing wink!

Precisely opposite the Residency is the handsome Dopper church, wherein the President regularly worshipped, and not infrequently himself ministered in holy things. The church is nearly new, and like much else in Pretoria is still unfinished. The four dials have indeed been duly placed on the four faces of the clock tower; but in that tower there is as yet no clock; and round those clock dials there move no clock hands. No wonder Pretoria with its dominant Dopper church, and its still more decidedly dominant Dopper President, mistook the true hour of its destiny, and madly made war precisely when peace was easiest of attainment. Kruger, dim-eyed and old, lived face to face continually with clock dials that betokened no progress, but, merely mocked the enquiring gaze. Which thing, the Chelsea Sage would say, was symbolical and significant of much!

In the centre of the before-mentioned Square is the large and usually crowded Dutch Reformed Church, doomed long ago, we were told, to be removed because of its exceeding unsightliness. Throughout the Transvaal in every town and hamlet, the House of God is invariably the central building, as also it is the centre of the most potent influence. In both Republics the minister was emphatically "a Master in Israel"; and in the welcome shadows of this great church I waited to witness one of the most interesting events of the century—the proclaiming of

Pretoria a British city by the official hoisting in it, as earlier in Bloemfontein, of the British flag; and by the stately "march past" of the British troops.

Facing me, on the side of the Square opposite to that occupied by the Palace of Justice, were the creditably designed Government Buildings, including the Raadsaal, which was surmounted by a golden figure of Liberty bearing in her hand a battle-axe and flag. On the forefront of the building in bold lettering there was graven the favourite Transvaal watchword, *eendract maakt magt*, which, being interpreted means, *right makes might*; and that motto, as every Britisher could see, precisely explained our presence there that day. Inside there still remained, in its accustomed place, the state chair of the departed President, in which, later on, I ventured to sit; and all around were ranged the, to me, eloquent seats of his departed senators. In that very hall, just nine months before, those senators, in secret session, had resolved to hurl defiance at the might of Britain; and so precipitated a war by which two sister Republics were, as such, hurried out of existence. Now the very corridors by which I approached that hall were crowded with Boers wearied with the fruitless fight, and eager to hand in their weapons.

In the waiting crowd outside I found a friend who courteously supplied me with a copy of a quite unique photograph— the only photograph taken of the solemn burial, a few hundred yards from where I stood, of a Union Jack, when that flag was hauled down in the Transvaal, and the British troops ingloriously retired. As shown in the photograph, over the grave was erected a slab, and on that slab was this most notable inscription:

In memory of the British flag in the Transvaal
which departed this life August 2nd, 1881 aged 4 years.
In other lands none knew thee but to love thee.
Resurgam

No such burial had the world seen before, and few bolder prophecies than that "I shall rise again," can be found in the history of any land; but a few minutes it became my memorable privilege to witness the actual fulfilment of that patriotic prediction. As in Johannesburg, so here, it was Lady Roberts' pocket edition of the *Union Jack* that was used; and we looked on excitedly; but the Statue of Liberty looked down benignly, while that tiny flag crept up nearer and nearer to its golden feet. Liberty has never anything to fear from the approach of that flag!

While in Pretoria the following story was told me by the soldier to whom it chiefly refers:

At the Orange River a corporal of the Yorkshire Light Infantry received a pocket copy of the *New Testament* from a Christian worker, and placed it in his tunic by the side of his field dressing. A godless man, who had been driven into the army by heavy drinking, he merely glanced at a verse or two, and then forgot its very presence in his pocket till he reached the battlefield of Graspan a few days later on. Then a Boer bullet passed right through the *Testament* and the dressing that lay beside it, was thereby deflected from its otherwise fatal course, and finally made a long surface wound on his right thigh. That wound he at once bound up with one of his putties, but for two hours was unable to stir from the place where he fell.

Then he managed to limp back to his battalion, and piteously begged his adjutant not to let his name be put down on the casualty list, for, said he, "my mother is in feeble health, and if she saw my name in the papers among the wounded she would worry herself almost to death, as years ago when she heard of my being hit in Tirah." That brave request was granted, and he remained in the ranks marching as one unwounded.

Yet neither this providential deliverance nor the terrors that soon followed at Modder River sufficed to lure to either prayer or praise this godless, but surely not graceless, corporal. On the 27th of August, however, which happened to be his thirtieth birthday, a devout sergeant had the joy of winning him to Christian decision; and that day, as he told me in Pretoria, he resolved to find out for himself whether after thirty years of misery the mercy of the Lord could provide for him thirty years of happiness.

On board the *Nubia*, amid piles of literature put on board for the amusement of the troops during the voyage, I discovered a quantity of pamphlets entitled *Beer Cellars and Beer Sellers*, the purpose of which was to prove that the beer sellers were England's most indispensable patriots; that the beer cellars were England's best citadels; and that the beer trade in general was the very backbone of England's stability. It was horribly tantalising to the men in face of such teaching to find that there had been placed on board for them not so much as a solitary barrel of this much belauded beverage. Through all the voyage every man remained perforce a total abstainer. Yet there was not a single death among those sixteen hundred, nor a solitary instance of serious sickness. What does Burton say to that?

As at sea, so on land, the authorities seemed more afraid of the beloved beer barrel than of the bullets of the Boers; and for the most part no countersign sufficed to secure for it admittance to our camps. An occasional tot of rum was distributed among the men; but even that seemed to be rather to satisfy a sentiment than to serve any really useful purpose. At any rate, some of the men, like myself, tramped all the way to Koomati Poort, often in the worst of weather, without taking a single tot, and were none the worse for so refraining, but rather so much the better.

The effect on the character of the men was still more remarkable; and while in Pretoria I was repeatedly assured that some who had been a perpetual worry to their officers in beer-ridden England, on the beerless *veldt*, or in the liquorless towns of the Transvaal, speedily took rank among the most reliable men in all their regiment. To my colleague, the Rev. W. Burgess, a major of the Yorkshires, said "Nineteen-twentieths of the crime in the British army is due to drink. As a proof I have been at this outpost with 150 men for six weeks, where we have absolutely no drink, and there have been only two minor cases brought before me. There is no insubordination whatever, and if you do away with drink you have in the British army an ideal army. Whether or not men can be made sober by Act of Parliament, clearly they can by martial law!"

With the men so sober, with a field-marshal so God-fearing, the constant outrages ascribed to them by slander-loving Englishmen at home, become a moral impossibility; and to that fact, after we had been long in possession of Pretoria, the principal minister of the Dutch Reformed Church in the Transvaal bore ready witness in the following letter sent by him to the Military Governor of Pretoria:

> Not a single instance of criminal assault or rape by non-commissioned officers or men of the British army on Boer women has come to my knowledge. I have asked several gentlemen and their testimony is the same. . . . The discipline and general moral conduct of His Majesty's troops in Pretoria is, under the circumstances, better than I ever expected it would or could be. There have certainly been cases of immoral conduct, but in no single instance, so far as I know, has force been used. They only go where they are invited and where they are welcome.
>
> *H. S. Bosman*

When such is the testimony of our adversaries, we need not hesitate to accept the similar tribute paid by Sir Redvers Buller to his army of abstainers in Natal:

> I am filled with admiration for the British soldiers, really the manner in which they have worked, fought, and endured during the last fortnight has been something more than human. Broiled in a burning sun by day, drenched in rain by night, lying but three hundred yards off an enemy, who shoots you if you show so much as a finger, they could hardly eat or drink by day; and as they were usually attacked by night, they got but little sleep; yet through it all they were as cheery and as willing as could be.

Men so devoted when on duty, don't transform themselves, the drink being absent, into incarnate demons when off duty; and no dominion, therefore, has more cause to be proud of its defenders than our own!

Chapter 10

Pretorian Impressions

Pretoria is manifestly a city in process of being made, and has probably in store a magnificent future, though at present the shanty and the palace stand cheek by jowl. Even the main roads leading into the town seemed atrociously bad as judged by English standards, and the paving of the principal streets was of a correspondingly perilous type. Yet the public buildings already referred to were not the only ones that claimed our commendation as signs of a progressive spirit. The Government Printing Works are remarkably handsome and complete; and while for educational purposes there is in Pretoria nothing quite comparable to Grey College at Bloemfontein, the secondary education of the late Republic's metropolis was well housed.

There is, however, one building provided for that purpose which has acquired an enduring interest of quite another kind, and which I visited, when it became a hospital, with very mingled emotions. The State's Model School, during the early stages of the war, was utilised as a prison for the British officers captured by the Boers. How keenly these brave men felt and secretly resented their ill-fortune they were too proud to tell, but one of the noblest of them had become, through the terrors of a disastrous fight, so piteously demented for a while that he actually wore hanging from his neck a piece of cardboard announcing that it was he who lost the guns at Colenso. Some of them would rather have lost their lives than in such fashion have lost their liberty, and the story which tells how three of them regained that liberty by escaping from this very prison is one of the most thrilling among all the records of the war. Most noted of the three is Winston Churchill, whose own graphic pen has told how he eluded the most vigilant search and finally reached the sea. But the adventures of Captain Haldane and his non-commissioned companion reveal yet more of daring and endurance. Captured at the same time as Churchill, and through the same cause—the disaster on November 13th to the armoured train at Chieveley—these two effected their escape long after the hue and cry on the heels of Churchill had died away. Within what was supposed to be a day or two of the removal of all the officers to a more secure "birdcage" outside the town, those two gentlemen vanished under the floor of their room, through a kind of tiny trap-door that I have often seen, but which was then partly concealed by a bed, and was apparently never noticed by their Boer custodians. In this prison beneath a prison, damp and dark and dismal beyond all describing, and where there was no room to stand erect, these two officers found themselves doomed to dwell, not for days merely, but for weeks. They were of course hunted for high and low, and sought in every conceivable place except the right place. Food was guardedly passed down to them by two or three brother officers who shared their secret, and at last, more dead than alive, they emerged from their dungeon the moment they discovered the building was deserted, and then daringly faced the almost hopeless, yet successful, endeavour to smuggle themselves to far-distant Delagoa Bay. Evidently the element of romance has not yet died out of this prosaic age!

Strangely sharing the fate of these British prisoners in this Model School was a godly and gifted minister of the Dutch Reformed Church. A Boer among Boers. He was never told why he was arrested by his brother Boers, and though kept under lock and key for months, he was never introduced to judge or jury. An advocate of peace, he was suspected of British leanings, and so almost before the war commenced rough hands were laid upon him. There was in the Transvaal a reign of terror. Secret service men were everywhere, and no one's reputation was safe, no one's position secure. In this land of newly-discovered gold men were driven to discover that the most golden thing of all was discreet silence on the part of those who differed from *the powers that be*. So he who simply sought to avert war was suspected of British sympathies, and to his unutterable surprise presently found himself the fellow prisoner of many a still more unfortunate British officer.

Of those officers, their character and intellectual attainments, he speaks in terms of highest praise. Their enforced leisure they devoted to various artistic and intellectual pursuits, and I have myself seen an admirably elaborate and accurate map of the Republics, covering the whole of a large classroom wall, drawn presumably from joint memory by these officers, who by its aid were able to trace the progress of the war as tidings filtered through to them by an ingenious system of signalling practised by sympathetic friends outside.

By those same officers this Dutchman was invited to become their unofficial chaplain, and he writes of the devotional services consequently arranged as among the chief delights of his life, the favourite hymn he says being the following:

Holy Father, in Thy mercy
Hear our anxious prayer.
Keep our loved ones, now far absent,
'Neath Thy care.

Jesus, Saviour, let Thy presence
Be their light and pride.
Keep, Oh keep them, in their weakness,
Near Thy side.

Holy Spirit, let Thy teaching
Sanctify their life.
Send Thy grace that they may conquer
In all strife.

It was to this much respected and much reviled predikant a Pretorian high official said: "We were determined to let it drift to a rupture with England, for then our dream would be realised of a Republic reaching to Table Mountain"; but surely such a song and such a scene in the State's Model School was a thing of which no man dreamed!

The private soldiers who like these, their officers, had become prisoners of war, were for greater security removed from their racecourse camp to a huge prison-pen at the Waterfall, some ten or twelve miles up the Pietersburg line. They numbered in all about three thousand eight hundred, and for a while fared badly at their captors' hands. But ultimately a small committee was formed in Pretoria and £5000 subscribed, to be spent in mitigating their lot and ministering in many ways to their comfort. In these ministrations of mercy the Wesleyan minister, whose grateful guest I for a while became, as afterwards of the genial host and hostess at the Silverton Mission Parsonage, took a prominent and much appreciated part as the following letter abundantly proves:

To the Rev. F. W. Macdonald
President
Wesleyan Church
London.
Pretoria
4th July 1900
Sir,—As chairman of a committee formed in January last for the purpose of assisting the British prisoners of war, I have been requested to bring officially to your notice the splendid work done by the Rev. H. W. Goodwin. From my position I have been thrown into intimate relationship with Mr Goodwin, and it is a great pleasure to me to testify to his invaluable services. I am not a member of your church, nor are my colleagues, but there is a unanimous desire among the British subjects that were permitted to remain in Pretoria, and who are therefore cognisant of Mr Goodwin's work, to place his record before you. It is our united hope that Mr Goodwin will receive some substantial mark of appreciation from the Church of which he is so fine a representative. I know of none finer in the highest sense in the Church which knows no distinction of forms or creeds.—I have the honour to be, Sir, your obedient servant,
J. Leigh Wood

On my arrival in Pretoria Mr Goodwin was at my request at once appointed as Acting Army Chaplain, and shortly after received the following most gratifying communication:

British Agency
Pretoria
9th June 1900
Dear Sir,—If you could kindly call on Lord Roberts some time today or tomorrow, it would give him great pleasure to meet one who has done so much for our prisoners of war.—Yours faithfully,
H. V. Conan
Lt.-Col., Mil. Sec.
The Rev. Goodwin

When Mr Goodwin accordingly called nothing could well exceed the warmth of the welcome and of the thanks the field-marshal graciously accorded him.

Among the prisoners at the Waterfall was a well-known Wesleyan sergeant of the 18th Hussars, who rallied around him all such as were of a devout spirit and became the recognised leader of the religious life of the prison camp. I therefore requested him to supply me with a brief statement of what in this respect had been done by the prisoners for the prisoners. He accordingly sent me the following letter:

Pretoria
7th July 1900
Reverend and Dear Sir,—Long before you asked me to write an account of the Christian work which was carried on from the 22nd of October 1899 to the 6th of June 1900, among the British prisoners of war at the Pretoria Racecourse, and afterwards at Waterfall, it had occurred to me that for the encouragement of other Christian workers particularly, and the members of the Church of Christ generally, some record should be made of the wonderful way in which God blessed us, and it is with the greatest pleasure that I accede to your request.
I was one of the 160 who were taken prisoners after the

battle of Talana Hill (Dundee), and a few days after arriving at our destination (Pretoria Racecourse) we heard some of our guard singing psalms and we immediately decided to ask the commandant for a tent for devotional purposes. It was given, and after the first few nights, till we were released by our own forces seven months afterwards, it was filled to overflowing nightly. On our being removed to Waterfall, we enlarged our tent to three times its original size, and later on we begged building material from the commandant, and built a very nice hall with a platform and seating accommodation for over 240. At last this became too small and we went into the open air twice a week, when no less than 500 to 700 congregated to hear the old, old story of Jesus and His love.

When we asked for the small tent we had no idea of the work growing as it did. We used to meet together every night, a simple gathering together of God's children, four in number, which increased to one hundred, with the Lord Himself as teacher. Then our comrades began to attend and we commenced to hold evangelistic services, which were continued to the end.

When we got to Waterfall we started a Bible-class and a prayer meeting, held alternately. The work was helped a great deal by other Christian brothers, without whose services, co-operation, fellowship and sympathy the work could hardly have been continued for any length of time. But, after all, speaking after the manner of men, our dear friend and pastor, the Rev. H.W. Goodwin, was the one who really enabled us to carry on the work. As the transport and commissariat are to any army, so Mr Goodwin was to us.

On our application, the Boer Government consented to allow the ministers of the various churches in Pretoria to visit us once a month for the purpose of conducting divine service. Of course such a privilege as this was greatly appreciated by the men, and one cannot help wondering why such restrictions were placed upon the ministers.

We had many cherished plans and bright hopes with regard

to the war, and when we were captured we found it hard to recognise the ordering of the Lord in our new conditions and unaccustomed circumstances; but we were taught some grand lessons, and we soon found that even imprisonment has its compensations; and we have to confess that His Presence makes the prison a palace. I have heard many thank God for bringing them to Waterfall gaol.

During the months we spent together we realised that God was blessing us in a most remarkable manner, and we may truly say that our fellowship was with the Father and with His Son Jesus Christ. Many backsliders were taught the folly of remaining away from the Father, and many were turned from darkness unto light. To Him be the glory.

On hearing of the near approach of our deliverers, and knowing that soon we should all part, we had a farewell meeting and many promised to write to me.

I received a number of letters ere we actually parted, but with the injunction *not to be opened till separated*, and from these I intend making a few extracts which lead me like the Psalmist to say "Because Thou hast been my help therefore in the shadow of Thy wings will I rejoice."

Of the extracts to which the sergeant refers it is impossible to give here more than a few brief samples; but even these may suffice to prove that our soldiers are by no means all, or mostly, sons of Belial, as their recent slanderers would have us believe.

A Bombardier of the 10th Mountain Battery writes—

I was brought to God on the 4th of February. I had often stood outside the tent and listened to the services, and one evening I went into the after-meeting and came away without Christ; but God was striving with me, and a few nights afterwards I realised that I was a hell-deserving sinner, and I cried unto God and He heard me; and that night I came away with Christ.

A Sergeant-Major of Roberts' Horse says—

I am indeed grateful to God for the loving-kindness He

has bestowed on me since my coming here as a prisoner of war. The meetings have been a great success and of the most orderly character.

A Sergeant of the Royal Irish Rifles adds—

Thanks be unto God, He opened my eyes on the night of the 21st of January 1900; and He has kept me ever since.

A Corporal of the Wilts., after telling of his capture at Rensberg, and his arrival at Waterfall, goes on to say—

I heard about the Gospel Tent from one of the Boer sentries, and I cannot express the happy feelings that passed through me when I saw the Christian band gathered together with one accord.

A Private of the Glosters relates the story of his own conversion, and then proceeds to say he shall never forget the meetings which were conducted by the Rev. H. W. Goodwin, especially the one in which he administered to them the blessed Sacrament. It was a Pentecostal time, and it pleased the Lord to add unto them eight souls that same night, and six the night following.

As the day of release drew near with all its inevitable excitement and unrest, certain British officers, themselves prisoners, were requested by the Boers to reside among these men at the Waterfall to ensure to the very last the maintenance of discipline; and the sanction of the Baptist minister who once conducted their parade service was sought by them for the singing of the following most touchingly appropriate hymn:

Lord a nation humbly kneeling
For her soldiers cries to Thee;
Strong in faith and hope, appealing
That triumphant they may be.
Waking, sleeping,
'Neath Thy keeping,
Lead our troops to victory.

Of our sins we make confession,
Wealth and arrogance and pride;

But our hosts, against oppression,
March with Freedom's flowing tide.
Father, speed them,
Keep them, lead them,
God of armies, be their guide.

Man of Sorrows! Thou hast sounded
Every depth of human grief.
By Thy wounds, Oh, heal our wounded.
Give the fever's fire relief.
Hear us crying
For our dying,
Of consolers be Thou chief.

Take the souls that die for duty
In Thy tender pierced hand;
Crown the faulty lives with beauty,
Offered for their Fatherland.
All forgiving,
With the living
May they in Thy kingdom stand.

And if Victory should crown us,
May we take it as from Thee
As Thy nation deign to own us;
Merciful and strong and free.
Endless praising
To Thee raising,
Ever Thine may England be!

Say their critics what they may, soldiers who compose such songs, and pen such testimonies, and conduct such services among themselves, seem scarcely the sort to let hell loose in South Africa!

Of the prisoners of war thus long detained in durance vile nearly a thousand were decoyed into a special train the night before the Guards' Brigade reached Pretoria. These deluded captives in their simplicity supposed they were being taken into the town to be there set at liberty; but instead of that they were hurried by, and, with the panic-stricken Boers, away and yet away, into their remotest eastern fastnesses, there presumably to be retained as long as possible as a sort of guarantee that the vastly larger number of Boers we held prisoners should be still generously treated by us. They might also prove useful in many ways if terms of peace came to be negotiated. So vanished for months their visions of speedy freedom!

The rest who still remained within the prison fence, and were, of course, still unarmed, three days later were cruelly and treacherously shelled by a Boer commando on a distant hill. The Boer guards detailed for duty at the prison had deserted their posts, and under the cover of the white flag, gone into Pretoria to surrender. Our men, therefore, who were practically free, awaiting orders, when thus unceremoniously shelled, at once stampeded; and late on Thursday night about nine hundred of them, footsore and famished, arrived at Mr Goodwin's house seeking shelter. He was apparently the only friend they knew in Pretoria, and to have a friend yet not to use him is, of course, absurd! So to his door they came in crowds, dragging with them the Boer Maxim gun, by which they had so long been overawed. While tea and coffee for all this host were being hurriedly prepared by their slightly embarrassed host, I sought permission from a staff officer to house the men for the night in our Wesleyan schoolrooms, and in the huge Caledonian Hall adjoining, which was at once commandeered for the purpose. I also requested that a supply of rations might at utmost speed be provided for them. Accordingly, not long before midnight a wagon arrived bringing by some fortunate misreading of my information, provisions, not for nine hundred hungry men, but for the whole three thousand prisoners whom we were supposed to have welcomed as our guests. It may seem incredible, but men who at that late hour had fallen fast asleep upon the floor, at the sound of that wagon's wheels suddenly awoke; and still more wonderful to tell, when morning came those nine hundred men, of the rations for three thousand, had left untouched only a few paltry boxes of biscuits. A hospital patient recently recovered from fever once said to me, "I haven't an appetite for two, sir; I have an appetite for ten!" And these released prisoners had evidently for that particular occasion borrowed the appetite of that particular patient!

The Caledonian Hall above referred to is a specially commodious building, and could not have been more admirably adapted for use as a Soldiers' Home if expressly erected for that purpose. It was accordingly commandeered by the military governor to be so used, and for months it was the most popular establishment in town or camp. At Johannesburg a Wesleyan and an Anglican Home were opened, both rendering excellent service; but as this was run on undenominational lines, it was left without a rival. It is a most powerful sign of the times that our military chiefs now unhesitatingly interest themselves in the moral and spiritual welfare of the men under their command. Some time before this Boer war commenced, on April 28, 1898, there was issued by the Commander-in-Chief of the British Army a memorandum which would have done no discredit to the Religious Tract Society if published as one of their multitudinous leaflets. A copy was supplied presumably to every soldier sent to Africa; and the first few sentences which refer to what may happily be regarded as steadily diminishing evils, read as follows:

It will be the duty of company officers to point out to the men under their control, and particularly to young soldiers, the *disastrous effect of giving way* to habits of intemperance and immorality. The excessive use of intoxicating liquors unfits the soldier for active work, blunts his intelligence, and is a fruitful source of military crime. The man who leads a vicious life *enfeebles his constitution* and exposes himself to the risk of contracting a disease of a kind which has of late made terrible ravages in the British army. Many men spend a great deal of the short time of their service in the military hospitals, the wards of which are crowded with patients, a large number of whom are permanently disfigured and incapacitated from earning a livelihood in or out of the army. Men tainted with this disease are *useless* while in the army and a burden to their friends after they have left it. Even those who do not altogether break down are unfit for service in the field, and would certainly be a source of weakness to their regiments, and a discredit to their comrades if employed in war.

Soldiers' Home at Pretoria

As one of the most effectual ways of combating these evils, and of providing an answer to the oft-repeated prayer, "Lead us not into temptation," Soldiers' Homes are now being so freely multiplied, that the Wesleyan Church has itself established over thirty, at a total cost of more than £50,000.

Some of those engaged in similar Christian work among the soldiers were gentlemen of ample private means who defrayed all their own expenses. Mr Anderson was thus attached to the Northumberland Fusiliers, and soon became a power for good among them. Mr and Mrs Osborn Howe did a really remarkable work in providing Soldiers' Homes, which followed the men from place to place over almost the entire field covered by our military operations, including Pretoria, and though they received quite a long list of subscriptions their own private resources have for years been freely placed at the Master's service, whether for work among soldiers or civilians.

When late on in the campaign it was intimated by certain officials that Lord Kitchener was not in sympathy with such work and would not grant such facilities for its prosecution as Lord Roberts had done, Mr Osborn Howe received the following reply to a letter of enquiry on that point:

> I am directed by Lord Kitchener to acknowledge the receipt of your letter of January 3rd. His Lordship much regrets that you should have been led to imagine that his attitude towards your work differs from that of Lord Roberts, and I am to inform you that so far from that being the case, he is very deeply impressed by the value of your work, and hopes that it may long continue and increase.
> Yours faithfully,
> *W. H. Congreve*
> Major, Private Secretary

Still more notable in this same connection is the fact that soon after Lord Roberts reached Cape Town to take supreme command, he caused to be issued the following most remarkable letter, which certainly marks a new departure in the usages of modern warfare, and carries us back in thought and spirit to the camps of

Cromwell and his psalm-singing Ironsides, or to the times when Scotland's Covenanters were busy guarding for us the religious light and liberty which are today our goodliest heritage.

Army Headquarters
Cape Town
January 23rd
Dear Sir,—I am desired by Lord Roberts to ask you to be so kind as to distribute to all ranks under your command the *Short Prayer for the use of Soldiers in the Field,* by the Primate of Ireland, copies of which I now forward. His Lordship earnestly hopes that it may be helpful to all of Her Majesty's soldiers who are now serving in South Africa.
Yours faithfully,
Neville Chamberlain
Colonel, Private Secretary
To the Commanding Officer

The Prayer

Almighty Father, I have often sinned against Thee. O wash me in the precious blood of the Lamb of God. Fill me with Thy Holy Spirit, that I may lead a new life. Spare me to see again those whom I love at home, or fit me for Thy presence in peace.
Strengthen us to quit ourselves like men in our right and just cause. Keep us faithful unto death, calm in danger, patient in suffering, merciful as well as brave, true to our Queen, our country, and our colours.
If it be Thy will, enable us to win victory for England, and above all grant us the better victory over temptation and sin, over life and death, that we may be more than conquerors through Him who loved us, and laid down His life for us, Jesus our Saviour, the Captain of the Army of God. *Amen*

The general who officially invited all his troops to use such a prayer could not fail to prove a warm friend and patron of Soldiers' Homes; and to the Pretoria Home he came, not merely formally to declare it open, but to attend one of the many concerts given there, thus encouraging by his example both the workers and those for whom they worked. A supremely busy and burdened man, *that* he made a part of his business; and surely he was wise, for one sober soldier is any day worth more than a dozen drunken ones.

The general who thus deliberately encouraged his troops to live devoutly, instead of being deemed by them on that account unsoldierly or fanatic, secured such a place in their confidence and affection as few even of the most magnetic leaders among men ever managed to obtain. The pet name by which they always spoke of him implied no approach to unseemly familiarity, but betokened the same kind of attachment as the veteran hosts of Napoleon the Great intended to express when they admiringly called their dread master the Little Corporal. He amply justified their confidence in him, and they amply justified his confidence in them; and so on resigning his command in South Africa he spoke of these "my comrades," as he called them, in terms as gratifying as they are uncommon:

> I am very proud that I am able to record, with the most absolute truth, that the conduct of this army from first to last has been exemplary. Not one single case of serious crime has been brought to my notice—indeed, nothing that deserves the name of *crime*. There has been no necessity for appeals or orders to the men to behave properly. I have trusted implicitly to their own soldierly feeling and good sense, and I have not trusted in vain. They bore themselves like heroes on the battlefield, and like gentlemen on all other occasions.

Lord Lytton tells us that in the days of Edward the Confessor the rage for psalm singing was at its height in England so that sacred song excluded almost every other description of vocal music: but though in South Africa a similar trend revealed itself among the troops, their camp fire concerts, and the concerts in the Pretoria Soldiers' Home, were of an exclusively secular type. At one which it was my privilege to attend, Lady Roberts and her daughters were present as well as the general, who generously arranged for a cigar to be given to every man in the densely crowded hall when the concert closed. All the songs were by members of the general's staff, and were excellent; but one, composed presumably by the singer, was topical and sensational in a high degree. It was entitled *Long as the World Goes Round*; and one verse assured us concerning "Brother Boer," with only too near an approach to truth,

> *He'll bury his mauser,*
> *And break all his vows, sir,*
> *Long as the world goes round!*

Another verse reminded us of a still more melancholy fact which yet awakened no little mirth. It was in praise of De Wet, who in spite of his blue spectacles, seemed by far the most clear-sighted of all the Boer generals, and who, notwithstanding his illiteracy, was beyond all others well versed in the bewildering ways of the *veldt*. He apparently had no skill for the conducting of set battles, but for ambushing convoys, for capturing isolated detachments, for wrecking trains, and for himself eluding capture when fairly ringed round with keen pursuers beyond all counting, few could rival him. Like hunted Hereward, he seemed able to escape through a rat hole, and by his persistence in guerrilla tactics not only seriously prolonged the war and enormously increased its cost, but also went far to make the desolation of his pet Republic complete. So there Lord Roberts sat and heard this sung by one of his staff:

> *Of all the Boers we have come across yet,*
> *None can compare with this Christian De Wet;*
> *For him we seem quite unable to get—*
> *(Though Hildyard and Broadwood,*
> *And our Soudanese Lord should)—*
> *Long as the world goes round!*

They *should* have got him, and they would have got him, if they could; but when Lord Roberts, long months after, set sail for home, he left De Wet still in the saddle. Then Kitchener, our Soudanese Lord, took up the running, and called on the Guards to aid him, but even they proved unequal to the hopeless task. "One pair of heels," they said, "can never overtake two pair of hoofs."

Then our picked mounted men monopolised the *tally-ho* to little better purpose. De Wet's guns were captured, his convoys cut off, but him no man caught, and possibly to this very day he is still complacently humming "Tommies may come and Tommies may go, but I trot on for ever."

The last verse of this sensational song had reference to yet another celebrity, but of a far more unsatisfactory type. All the earlier part of that Thursday I had spent in the second Raadsaal, attending a court-martial on one of our prisoners of war, Lieutenant Hans Cordua, late of the Transvaal State Artillery, who, having surrendered, was suffered to be at large on parole. In my presence he pleaded guilty, first to having broken his parole in violation of his solemn oath; secondly, to having attempted to break through the British lines disguised in British khaki, in order to communicate treasonably with Botha; and thirdly, to having conspired with sundry others to set fire to a certain portion of Pretoria with a view to facilitating a simultaneous attempt to kidnap Lord Roberts and all his staff. Cordua was with difficulty persuaded to withdraw the plea of guilty, so that he might have the benefit of any possible flaw his counsel could detect in the evidence; but in the end the death sentence was pronounced, confirmed, and duly executed in the garden of Pretoria Gaol on August 24th. It was from that court-martial I came to the Soldiers' Home Concert, sat close behind Lord Roberts, and listened to this song:

Though the Boer some say is a practised thief,
Yet it certainly beggars all belief,
That he slimly should try to steal our Chief.
But no Hollander mobs
Shall kidnap our Bobs
Long as the world goes round!

Historians tell us that the hospital arrangements in some of our former wars were by no means free from fault. Hence Steevens in his *Crimean Campaign* asserts that while the camp hospitals absolutely lacked not only candles, but medicines, wooden legs were supplied to them from England so freely that there were finally four such legs for every man in hospital. Clearly those wooden legs were consigned by wooden heads.

Even in this much better managed war the fever epidemic at Bloemfontein, combined with a month of almost incessant rain, overtaxed for a while, as we have seen, the resources and strength and organizing skill of a most willing and fairly competent medical staff.

But Pretoria was plagued with no corresponding epidemic, and possessed incomparably ampler supplies, which were drawn on without stint. In addition to the Welsh, the Yeomanry, and other canvas hospitals planted in the suburbs, the splendid Palace of Justice was requisitioned for the use of the Irish hospital, which, like several others, was fitted out and furnished by private munificence. The principal school buildings were also placed at the disposal of the medical authorities, and were promptly made serviceable with whatever requisites the town could supply. To find suitable bedding, however, for so vast a number of patients was a specially difficult task. All the rugs and tablecloths the stores of the town contained were requisitioned for this purpose; green baize and crimson baize, repp curtains and plush, anything, everything remotely suitable, was claimed and cut up to serve as quilts and counterpanes, with the result that the beds looked picturesquely, if not grotesquely, gay. One ward, into which I walked, was playfully called *the menagerie* by the men that occupied it, for on every bed was a showy rug, and on the face of every rug was woven the figure of some fearsome beast, Bengal tigers and British lions being predominant. It was in appearance a veritable lion's den, where our men dwelt in peace like so many modern Daniels, and found not harm but health and healing there.

In this campaign the loss of life and vigour caused by sickness was enormously larger than that accounted for by bullet wounds and bayonets. At the Orange River, just before the Guards set out on their long march, thirty Grenadier officers stretched their legs under their genial colonel's "mahogany," which consisted of rough planks supported on biscuit boxes. Of those only nine were still with us when we reached Pretoria, and of the nine several had been temporarily disabled by sickness or wounds. The battalion at starting was about a thousand strong, and afterwards received various drafts amounting to about four hundred more; but only eight hundred marched into Pretoria. The Scots Guards, however, were so singularly fortunate as not to lose a single officer during the whole campaign.

The non-combatants in this respect were scarcely less unfortunate than the bulk of their fighting comrades. A band of workers in the service of the Soldiers' Christian Association set out together from London for South Africa. There were six of them, but before the campaign was really half over only one still remained at his post. My faithful friend and helper, whom I left as army scripture reader at Orange River, after some months of devoted work was compelled to hasten home. A similar fate befell my Canadian, my Welsh, and one of my Australian colleagues. The highly esteemed Anglican chaplain to the Guards, who steadily tramped with them all the way to Pretoria and well earned his D.S.O., was forbidden by his medical advisers to proceed any further, and his successor, Canon Knox Little, whose praise as a preacher is in all the churches, found on reaching Koomati Poort that his strength was being overstrained, and so at once returned to the sacred duties of his English Canonry. Thus to many a non-combatant the medical staff was called to minister, and the *veldt* to provide a grave.

The presence of skilled lady-nurses in these Hospitals was of immense service, not merely as an aid to healing, but also as a refining and restraining influence among the men. In this direction they habitually achieved what even the appearing of a chaplain did not invariably suffice to accomplish. It was the cheering experience of Florence Nightingale repeated on a yet wider scale. In her army days oaths were greatly in fashion. The expletives of one of even the Crimean *generals* became the jest of the camp; and when later in his career he took over the Aldershot Command, it was laughingly said "he *swore* himself in"; which doubtless he did in a double sense. Yet men trained in habits so evil when they came into the Scutari Hospital ceased to swear and forgot to grumble. Said the Lady with the Lamp:

> Never came from one of them any word, or any look, which a gentleman would not have used, and the tears

came into my eyes as I think how amid scenes of loathsome disease and death, there rose above it all the innate dignity, gentleness and chivalry of the men.

Now as then there are other ministries than those of the pulpit; and hospitals in which such influences exert themselves, may well prove, in more directions than one, veritable *houses of healing*.

As illustrating how gratefully these men appreciate any slightest manifestation of interest in their welfare, mention may here be made of what I regard as the crowning surprise of my life. At the close of an open air parade service in Pretoria a sergeant of the Grenadiers stepped forward, and in the name of the non-commissioned officers and men of that battalion presented to me, in token of their goodwill, a silver pencil case and a gold watch. I could but reply that the goodwill of my comrades was to me beyond all price, and that this golden manifestation of it, this gift coming from such a source, I should treasure as a victorious fighting man would treasure a V.C.

The kindnesses lavished on our soldiers, as far as circumstances would permit, throughout the whole course of this campaign, by civilian friends at home, in the Colonies, and in the conquered territories, defy all counting and all description. In some cases, indeed, valuable consignments intended for their comfort seem never to have reached their destination, but the knowledge that they were thus thought of and cared for had upon the men an immeasurable influence for good. Later on, even the people of Delagoa Bay sent a handsome Christmas hamper to every blockhouse between the frontier and Barberton, while at the same time the King of Portugal presented a superb white buck, wearing a suitably inscribed silver collar, to the Cornwalls who were doing garrison duty at Koomati Poort. But in Pretoria, where among other considerations my Wesleyan friends regularly provided a Saturday "Pleasant Hour," the soldiers in return invited the whole congregation to a "social," on which they lavished many a pound, and which they made a brilliant success. It was a startling instance of soldierly gratitude; and illustrates excellently the friendly attitude of the military and of the local civilians towards each other.

It sometimes happened among these much enduring men that the greater their misery the greater their mirth. Thus our captured officers, close guarded in the Pretoria Model School, and carefully cut off from all the news of the day, amused themselves by framing parodies on the absurd military intelligence published in the local Boer papers; whereof let the following verse serve as a sample:

Twelve thousand British were laid low;
One Boer was wounded in the toe.
Such is the news we get to know
In prison.

About this time there came into my hands a sample copy of *The Ladysmith Lyre*; but clearly though the last word in its title was perfectly correct as a matter of pronunciation the spelling was obviously inaccurate. It was a merry invention of news during the siege by men who were hemmed in from all other news; and so the grosser the falseness the greater the fun. In my own particular copy I found the following dialogue between two Irish soldiers:

First Private—"The captain told me to keep away from the enemy's foire!"
Second Private—"What did you tell the Captain?"
First Private—"I told him the Boers were so busy shelling they hadn't made any foire!"

That is scarcely a brilliant jest; but then it was begotten amid the agonies of the siege.

One of the poems published in this same copy of *The Ladysmith Lyre* has in it more of melancholy than of mirth. It tells of the hope deferred that maketh the heart sick; and gives us a more vivid idea than anything else yet printed of the secret distress of the men who saved Natal—a distress which we also shared. It is entitled—

AFTER EDGAR ALLAN POE

Once upon a midnight dreary, while I pondered, weak and weary,
Over all the quaint and curious yarns we've heard about the war,

Suddenly there came a rumour—(we can always take a few more)
Started by some chap who knows more than the others knew before:
"We shall see the reinforcements in another—month or more!"
Only this and nothing more!

But we're waiting still for Clery, waiting, waiting, sick and weary
Of the strange and silly rumours we have often heard before.
And we now begin to fancy there's a touch of necromancy,
Something almost too uncanny, in the unregenerate Boer—
Only this and nothing more!

Though our hopes are undiminished that the war will soon be finished,
We would be a little happier if we knew a little more.
If we had a little fuller information about Buller;
News about Sir Redvers Buller, and his famous Army Corps;
Information of the General and his fighting Army Corps.
Only this and nothing more!

And the midnight shells uncertain, whistling through the
night's black curtain,
Thrill us, fill us with a touch of horror never felt before.
So to still the beating of our hearts, we kept repeating
"Some late visitor entreating entrance at the chamber door,
This it is; and nothing more!"

Oh how slow the shells come dropping, sometimes bursting,
sometimes stopping,
As though themselves were weary of this very languid war.
How distinctly we'll remember all the weary dull November;
And it seems as if December will have little else in store;
And our Christmas dinner will be bully beef and plain stickfast.
Only this and nothing more!

Letham, Letham, tell us truly if there's any news come newly;
Not the old fantastic rumours we have often heard before—
Desolate yet all undaunted! Is the town by Boers still haunted?
This is all the news that's wanted—tell us truly we implore—
Is there, is there a relief force? Tell us, tell us, we implore!
Only this and nothing more.

For we're waiting rather weary! Is there such a man as Clery?
Shall we ever see our wives and mothers, or our sisters and our brothers?

Shall we ever see those others, who went southwards long before?
Shall we ever taste fresh butter? Tell us, tell us, we implore!
We are answered—nevermore!

When twenty months later the Scots Guards again found themselves in Pretoria they too began dolorously to enquire, "Shall we ever see our wives and mothers, or our sisters and our brothers?" But meanwhile much occurred of which the following chapters are a brief record.

CHAPTER 11

Pretoria to Belfast

On reaching Pretoria, almost unopposed, our Guardsmen jumped to the hasty and quite unjustifiable conclusion that the campaign was closing, and that in the course of about another fortnight some of us would be on our homeward way. They forgot that after a candle has burned down into its socket it may still flare and flicker wearisomely long before it finally goes out. War lights just such a candle, and no extinguisher has yet been patented for the instant quenching of its flame just when our personal convenience chances to clamour for such quenching. Indeed, the "flare and flicker" period sometimes proves, where war is concerned, scarcely less prolonged, and much more harassing, than the period of the full-fed flame. So Norman William found after the battle of Hastings. So Cromwell proved when the fight at Worcester was over. So the Americans discovered when they had captured Manila. Our occupation of Bloemfontein by no means made us instant masters of the whole Free State, and our presence in Pretoria we had yet to learn was not at all the same thing as the undisputed possession of the entire Transvaal. Indeed, the period that actually interposed between the two, proved the longest "fortnight" ever recorded.

How that came about, however, is made quite clear by the following extract from the High Commissioner's despatches:

If it had been possible for us to screen those portions of the conquered territory, which were fast returning to peaceful pursuits, from the incursions of the enemy still in the field, a great deal of what is now most deplorable in the condition of South Africa would never have been experienced. The vast extent of the country, the necessity of concentrating our forces for the long advance, first to Pretoria and then to Koomati Poort, resulted in the country already occupied being left open to raids, constantly growing in audacity, and fed by small successes, on the part of a few bold and skilful guerrilla leaders who had nailed their colours to the mast.

The reappearance of these disturbers of the peace, first in the south-east of the Orange River Colony, then in the south-west of the Transvaal, and finally in every portion of the conquered territory, placed those of the inhabitants who wanted to settle down in a position of great difficulty. Instead of being made prisoners of war, they had been allowed to remain on their farms on taking the oath of neutrality, and many of them were really anxious to keep it. But they had not the strength of mind, nor from want of education, a sufficient appreciation of the sacredness of the obligation which they had undertaken, to resist the pressure of their old companions in arms when these reappeared among them appealing to their patriotism and to their fears. In a few weeks or months the very men whom we had spared and treated with exceptional leniency were up in arms again, justifying their breach of faith in many cases by the extraordinary argument that we had not preserved them from the temptation to commit it.

Early in the long halt near Pretoria, at Silverton Camp, the Guards' Brigade was formally assembled to hear read a telegram from H.R.H. The Prince of Wales, congratulating them on the practical termination of the war; whereupon as though by positive prearrangement the Boers plumped a protesting shell in startlingly close proximity to where our cheering ranks not long before had stood. It was the Boer way of saying "bosh" to our ill-timed boast that the war was over.

Botha and his irreconcilables were at this time occupying a formidable position, with a frontage of fifteen miles, near

Pienaar's Poort, where the Delagoa line runs through a gap in the hills, fifteen miles east of Pretoria; and this position Lord Roberts found it essential to attack with 17,000 men and seventy guns on Monday, June 11th, that is just a week after the neighbouring capital had surrendered. The fighting extended over three days; French attacking on our left, Hamilton on our right, and Pole Carew in the centre keenly watching the development of these flanking movements. In the course of this stubborn contest the invisible Boers did for one brief while become visible, as they galloped into the open in hope of capturing the Q Battery, which had already won for itself renown by redeeming Sanna's Post from complete disaster. Then it was Hamilton ordered the memorable cavalry charge of the 12th Lancers, which saved the guns, and scattered the Boers, but cost us the life of its gallant and God-fearing Colonel Lord Airlie, who before the war greatly helped me in my work at Aldershot. The death of such a man made the battle of Diamond Hill a mournfully memorable one; for Lord Airlie combined in his own martial character the hardness of the diamond with its lustrous pureness; and his last words just before the fatal bullet pierced his heart, were said to be a characteristic rebuke of an excited and perhaps profane sergeant: "Pray, moderate your language!" Wholesome advice, none too often given, and much too seldom heeded!

As the inevitable result of this further fighting, the men who had fondly hoped to be shortly on their way to Hyde Park Corner, suffered just then from a severe attack of heart-sickness, which was none other than a passing spasm of home-sickness! "Home, sweet home" sighed they, "and we never knew how sweet till now"! Meanwhile, however, we were wonderfully well supplied with home news, for within a single fortnight no less than 360 sacks of letters and various postal packets reached the Guards' Brigade, in spite of whole mails being captured by the Boers, and hosts of individual letters or parcels having gone hopelessly astray. Official reports declare that a weekly average of nearly 750,000 postal items were sent from England to the army in South Africa throughout the whole period covered by the war, so that it is quite clear we were not forgotten by loved ones far away, and the knowledge of that fact afforded solace, if not actual healing, even for those whose heart-sickness was most acute.

Early in July, the commander-in-chief had accumulated sufficient supplies, and secured sufficient remounts, to make a further advance possible. On the 7th, the Boers were pushed back by Hutton to Bronkers Spruit, where as the sequel of the Diamond Hill fight on June 12th, the Australians had surprised and riddled a Boer laager. While however Botha was thus sullenly retreating eastward, he secretly despatched a strong detachment round our left wing to the north-west of Pretoria under the leadership of Delarey, who on the 11th flung himself like a thunderbolt out of a clear sky on a weak post at Nitral's Nek, and there captured two guns with 200 prisoners. On July 16th, Botha himself once more attacked our forces, but was again driven off by Generals Pole Carew and Hutton; and the surrender on the 29th of General Prinsloo, with over 4000 Boers and three guns in the Orange River Colony, secured our remoter lines of communication from a very formidable menace, so clearing the course for another onward move.

On Tuesday, July 24th, the Guards' Brigade said goodbye to Donkerhook, where their camp had become a fixture since the fight on Diamond Hill, and where their conduct once more won my warmest admiration. In the very midst of that camp, in which so many thousands of men tarried so long, were sundry farmhouses, and *Kaffir* homes, the occupants of which were never molested from first to last, nor any of their belongings touched, except as the result of a perfectly voluntary sale and purchase. Indeed, the identic day we left, turkeys, geese, ducks, and other "small deer," were still wandering round their native haunts, none daring to make them afraid. The owners had declined to sell; and our ever hungry men had honourably refrained from laying unpermitted hands on these greatly enjoyable dainties. Such honesty in a hostile land, in relation to the property of a hostile peasantry, made me marvel; and still more when maintained in places where unmistakable treachery had been practised as in this identic neighbourhood.

At Wolmaran's pleasant country house, close beside our camp, the white flag flew, and there our general took up his abode. Some members of this well-known family were still out on commando, but those that remained at home eagerly surrendered all arms, were profuse in professions of friendliness, and were duly pledged to formal neutrality. But a recent Transvaal law had reduced the wages of all *Kaffirs* from about twenty shillings to a uniform five shillings a week, and Wolmaran's unpaid or ill-paid negroes revenged themselves by revealing their master's secrets. Partly as the result of hints thus obtained, we found hidden in his garden over thirty rifles, the barrel of a Maxim gun, and about £10,000 in gold—presumably Government money; also a splendid supply of provisions was discovered—presumably Government stores; and in the family cemetery there was dug up a quantity of dynamite. The gentleman who thus gave up his arms, and in this fashion kept his oath, at once became our prisoner, but his house and its contents remained untouched. And when we left, some of his barndoor fowls were still there to see us off!

This is a notable but typical illustration of the way in which, with unwise leniency, surrendered burghers were allowed access to our camps, and recompensed our reliance on their honour by revealing our secrets to our foes, and, when they dared, unearthing their buried arms to level them once more at our too confiding troops.

A march of fifteen or eighteen miles brought us to Bronkhorst Spruit, the scene of a dastardly massacre in December 1880, of the men of the Connaught Rangers, who, ere yet there was any declaration of war, were marching with their wives and children from Lydenburg to Pretoria. I stood bareheaded beside one of the mounds that hide their bones, close to the roadside where they fell, and bethought me of the strange Providence through which, nearly twenty years after the event, there was now marching past those very graves a vast avenging army on its way to those same mountain fastnesses whence our murdered comrades of the long ago set out on their fatal journey. Sowing and reaping are often far apart; but there is no sundering them!

At our mess dinner that same evening the conversation turned to the kindred, but still more shameful deed recently devised, though happily in vain, at Johannesburg. There Cordua had indeed been out-Corduad by a conspiracy to assassinate in cold blood all the military officers attending some sports about to be held under military patronage at the racecourse. About eighty of the conspirators were captured in the very act of completing their plans. Nearly three hundred more were said to be implicated, and being chiefly of foreign extraction were quietly sent out of the country. It was the biggest thing in plots, and the wildest, that recent years have seen outside Russia.

One often wonders how it comes to pass that people so demonstratively religious prove in so many cases conspicuously devoid of truth and honour and common honesty; but various explanations, each setting forth some partial contributory cause, may easily be conceived.

As among Britons, so among Boers, there are, as a matter of course, varying degrees of loyalty to the moral law, and of sincerity in religious profession. It is therefore manifestly unfair to condemn a whole people because of individual immoralities. The outrageous deeds just described may well have been in large part the work of "lewd fellows of the baser sort," a sort of which the Transvaal has unfortunately no monopoly, and of which the better type of Boer scorns to become the apologist. Moreover, Johannesburg drew to itself with a rush a huge number not only of honourable adventurers, but also of wastrels, representing every class and clime under heaven. Many of these were commandeered or volunteered for service on the Boer side when war broke out, and by their lawlessnesses proved almost as great a terror to their friends as to their foes. Young Cordua was of foreign birth, and there were few genuine Boers among the Johannesburg conspirators; but it was the Transvaal they blindly sought to serve; and so on the shoulders of the whole Transvaal community is laid, none too justly, the entire blame for such mistakes.

Then too, however mistakenly, I cannot but think the peculiar type of piety cherished by the Boers is largely responsible for the moral obliquity of which, justly or unjustly, I heard complaints continually from those who professed to know them well. These sons of the Huguenots and of the Dutch refugees who fled from the persecuting zeal of Alva have all sprung from an exceptionally religious stock, and with dogged conservatism still cling to the rigid traditions and narrow beliefs of a bygone age. The country-bred Boer resembles not remotely our own Puritans and Covenanters. He and his are God's Elect, and the Elect of the Lord have ever seemed prone to take liberties with the law of the Lord. They deem themselves a chosen race to whom a new Canaan has been divinely given, and in defence of whom Jehovah Himself is bound to fight. At the commencement of the campaign it was common talk that "they had commandeered the Almighty." Their piety and practice are largely modelled on Old Testament lines. They used God's name and quoted Scripture *ad nauseam* even in State correspondence. Their President was also their High Priest; yet in business transactions they were reputed to be as slim as Jacob in his dealings with Laban; and a lack of loyalty to the exact truth, some of their own clergy say, had become almost a national characteristic. "The bond-slave of my mere word I will never be" has often been quoted as a Boer proverb; and those that had lived long in the land assured me that proverb and practice too commonly keep company.

It is a perilous thing for men or nations to deem themselves in any exclusive sense Heaven's favourites. Such conceptions do not minister to heavenly-mindedness, or beget lives of ethic beauty. The ancient Hebrews, blinded by this very belief, became "worse than the heathen," and herein lies a solemn warning alike for the beaten Boer and the boastful Briton! There is no true religion where there is no all round righteousness; and wheresoever that is wanting the wrath of God cannot but abide.

Our next day's march ended just as a heavy thunderstorm with still heavier rain broke upon us; so the Grenadier officers pitched their mess as close as they could get to the sheltering wall of a decidedly stenchful *Kaffir* cottage. There we stood in the drenching wet and ate our evening meal, which was lunch and dinner in one. In that one-roomed cottage, with a smoking fire on the floor and a heap of mealie corn-cobs in the corner, there slept that night two *Kaffir* men, one *Kaffir* woman, four *Kaffir* piccaninnies, four West Australian officers, one officer of the Guards on the corn-cobs, a quantity of live poultry, and a dead goat; its sleep, of course, being that from which there is no awaking. That they were not all stifled before morning is astonishing, but the fact remains that the goat alone failed to greet the dawn.

Nearly every man in the camp was that night soaked to the skin, and for once the Guards made no attempt to sing at or to sing down the storm. As they apologetically explained at breakfast time, they were really "too down on their luck" to try. But with my usual good fortune I managed to pass the night absolutely dry, and that too without borrowing a corner of that horrid *Kaffir* cottage. The next night found us at Brugspruit, close to a colliery, where we stayed a considerable while, and managed to house ourselves in comparative comfort, that gradually became near akin to luxury. Here the junior officers courteously assisted me to shovel up an earthen shelter, with a sheet of corrugated iron for a roof, and thus protected I envied no millionaire his marble halls, though my blankets were sometimes wet with evening dew, and the ground white with morning frost.

During the long halt of the Grenadiers at Brugspruit, the Scots Guards remained at Balmoral, moving thence to Middelburg, and one of the Coldstream battalions was detailed to guard the Oliphant River, station, and bridge, which I crossed when on my way to Middelburg to conduct a Sunday parade service there; but at the river station the train tarried too brief a while and the battalion was too completely hidden on the far side of a rough *kopje* to permit my gaining even a passing glance of their camp. In South Africa full often the so-called sheep and their appointed shepherd found themselves thus unwittingly forbidden to see each others' face.

A little later on we found the line in possession, not of the Boers, but of a big drove of horses which seemed bent on proving that they could outdo even the Boers themselves in the rapidity of their retreat before an advancing foe. Mile after mile they galloped, but mile after mile they kept to the track, just in front of our engine, which whistled piercingly and let off steam as though in frantic anger. Presently we slowed down almost to a walking pace, for we had no wish to spill the blood or crush the bones of even obstructive horses. But as we slowed our pace they provokingly slackened theirs, and when once more we put on steam they did the same. So in sheer desperation our guard dismounted and ran himself completely out of breath, while he pelted the nearest of the drove with stones, and sought to scare it with flourishes of his official cap. But that horse behaved like a dull-headed ass, and cared no more for the waving of official caps than for the wild screaming of our steam whistle. We were losing time horribly fast because our pace was thus made so horribly slow. Finally a pilot engine came down from Middelburg to ascertain what had become of our long belated train, and this unlooked for movement from the rear fortunately proved too much for the nerves of even such determined obstructionists. It scared them as effectually as a flanking movement scared the Boers. They broke in terror from the line and, Boerlike, vanished.

Middelburg we found to be a thriving village, which will probably grow into an important town when the mineral wealth of the district is in due time developed. At present the principal building is as usual the Dutch Reformed Church, the pastor of which had forsaken the female portion of his flock to follow the fortunes of the fighting section. There are also two good-sized Dopper churches, which habitually remain void and empty all the year round, except on one Sunday in each quarter, when the farmer folk come from near and far to hold a fair, and to celebrate the Sacrament of the Lord's Supper—"The night meal," as they appropriately call it. These are the four great events of the Dopper year, and of this tiny city's business life.

The Dopper is the ultra Boer of South Africa, the Puritan of Puritans, the Covenanter of Covenanters, whose religious creed and conduct are compacted of manifold rigidities, and who would deem it as unpardonable a sin to shave off his beard, as it would have been for an early Methodist preacher to wear one. Formerly Doppers and Methodists both piously combed their hair over their foreheads, and clipped it in a straight line just above the eyebrows. But alas! in this as in many other directions,

Methodists and Doppers have alike become "subject to vanity." In these degenerate days "the fringe" has flitted from the masculine to the feminine brow; and now that it is "crinkled" no longer claims to be a badge of superior sanctity. In one of these Dopper churches the Rev. W. Frost long conducted Wesleyan services, the crowding troops having made our own church far too small.

The other, on the occasion of my first visit, was occupied by Canon Knox Little, who there conducted the Anglican parade service, and preached with great fervour from the very pulpit whence, some months before, President Kruger had delivered a discourse presumably of a decidedly different type. But the Wesleyan church immediately adjoining the camping ground of the 2nd Coldstream battalion, which I had the privilege that day of reopening, was at a later period used for a brief while by the Roman Catholic chaplains. War is a strange revolutionist if not always a reformer.

The next day, which was August Bank Holiday, I returned in safety to Brugspruit, but only to discover that in those parts even railway travelling had become a thing of deadly peril. I there saw two trains just arrived from Pretoria, the trucks filled with remount horses and cavalry men on their way to join General French's force. The first engine bore three bullet holes in its encasing water tank, holes which the driver had hastily plugged with wood, so preventing the loss of all his water and the fatal stoppage of the train. Several of the trucks were riddled with bullet-holes, and in one I saw a dead horse, shot, lying under the feet of its comrades; while in another truck, splashed with great clots of blood, similarly lay yet another horse almost dead. Several more were wounded but still remained upon their feet, and still had before them a journey of many miles ere their wounds could receive attention, or the living be severed from the dead. For horses this has been a specially fagging and fatal war, and for them there are no well-earned medals!

The second engine bore kindred bullet holes in its water tank. A shot had smashed the glass in the window of the break-van in which some officers were travelling; and in one of the trucks I was shown a hole in the thick timber made by a bullet, which, after passing through two inches of wood, had pierced a lancer's breast and killed him, besides shattering the wrist of yet another lancer. Those trains had just been fired at by a mounted Boer patrol which had caught our men literally napping. Most of them were lying fast asleep in the bottom of the trucks, with their unloaded carbines beside or under them, so that not a solitary reply shot was fired as the trains sped past the point of peril.

After repeated disasters of this kind had occurred, orders were issued forbidding men to travel in such careless and unguarded fashion; while all journeying that was not indispensible was peremptorily stopped! My own contemplated visit to Pretoria next day was consequently postponed till there came some more urgent call or some more convenient season.

On this part of the line the troops had often to be their own stokers and drivers, with the result that sniping Boers were not the only peril a passenger had to fear. From Dalmanutha in those delightsome days a train was due to start as usual with one engine behind and one in front. The driver of the leading engine blew his whistle and opened his regulator. The driver of the back engine did the same, but somehow the train refused to move. It was supposed the breaks were on, but it was presently discovered that the rear engine had reversed its gear, and there had thus commenced a tug of war—the one engine pulling its hardest against the other and neither winning a prize. In those days railway life became rich in comedies and tragedies, especially the latter, whereof let one further illustration of much later date, as described by Mr Burgess, suffice:

At Heidelberg on Thursday, March 7th, at ten o'clock in the morning there was a loud report as of a gun firing from one of the forts; but it was soon known that it was an explosion of dynamite on the line about a mile and a half from the railway station. The Boers had evidently placed dynamite under the metals, and it is supposed that while they were doing this, a number of them came down and engaged the outposts, and that was the firing that was heard in the town. A flat trolley with a European ganger and seven coolies and natives went over the first mine without exploding it; but on reaching the second, about a mile beyond, an explosion took place. The ganger after being blown fifty feet, escaped most miraculously with only a few bruises. Sad to relate three Indians were blown to pieces so as hardly to be recognised, and two others were seriously hurt. Immediately after this first explosion, a construction train left the Heidelberg railway station, and exploded the mine which the trolley had failed to explode; but fortunately very little damage was done as they had taken the precaution to place a truck in front of the engine. The second explosion occurred about a mile from the station and was plainly visible to those standing on the platform.

On setting out a second time from Brugspruit for Middleburg to conduct the Sunday services there, I was astonished to find the train consisted of about a dozen trucks, some open, some closed, but all filled to overflowing with Dutch women and Dutch children of every sort and size. Flags were fluttering from almost every truck, no khaki man carrying arms was suffered to travel by that train, and when the Roman Catholic chaplain and myself entered the break-van we seemed to be taking charge of a gigantic Mothers' Meeting out for a holiday, babies and all, or else to be escorting a big Sunday School to "Happy Hampstead" for its annual treat. It was the second large consignment of the sort which General Botha had consented to receive, and of which we were anxious to be rid. They were some of the wives and offspring of his fighting men, and were in most cases foodless, friendless, dependent for their daily bread on British bounty. It was therefore more fitting their own folk should feed them, as they were abundantly able and willing to do. Moreover, among them were women who had acted as spies, while others had hidden arms in their homes, so that to us they had become a serious peril, as well as a serious expense. We were consequently glad to be quit of them, and sincerely regretted that the capture of Barberton later on made us again their custodians.

Our first parade service next morning was held in the Wesleyan church, and was followed by open-air worship in the outlying encampment of the Scots Guards. The evening voluntary service was delightfully hearty and delightfully well attended. But most of the afternoon was spent at the railway station waiting for and watching the arrival of yet another train load of women and children on their way to realms beyond! Seven-and-twenty truck loads presently reached Middelburg in most defiant mood, for they waved their home-made Transvaal flags in our faces; they had bedecked themselves with Transvaal ribbons and Transvaal rosettes almost from head to foot. They shaded their faces with parasols in which the four Transvaal colours were combined; and they sang with every possible variety of discordancy Transvaal hymns, especially the Transvaal national anthem. But unless these gentle ladies can cook and stitch vastly better than they seemed able to sing, their husbands and brothers are much to be pitied.

Their patriotism was so pronounced and aggressive that they literally spat at the soldiers, and assured them that no money of theirs would ever suffice to purchase the paltriest flag they carried. The seeds of ill-will and hate for all things British had been planted in the mind and heart of almost every Boer child long before the war began, but those seeds ripened rapidly, and the reaping bids fair to be prolonged.

Before this weary conflict came to a close, nearly every Boer family was gathered in from the perils and privations of the war-wasted *veldt*; and so, while nearly 30,000 burghers were detained as prisoners of war at various points across the sea, their wives and children, to the number of over 100,000, were tenderly cared for in English laagers all along the line of rails or close to conveniently situated towns. Slanderous statements have been made as to the treatment meted out to these unfortunates, for which my visits revealed no warrant; but of more value is the testimony of one of their own church officials, who carefully inspected the women's refuge camp at Port Elizabeth, and reported the result to the local Intelligence Department. This deacon of the Dutch Reformed Church, Mr T. J. Ferreira, says:

I came down here on hearing of the reports at Steytlerville of the bad treatment the women exiles are receiving from the military. I was determined to find out the truth, and publish same in the Dutch and English papers. I stayed in the camp all day, and dined with the exiles. The food was excellent—I had roast lamb, soup, potatoes, bread, coffee, and biscuits. All was well cooked and perfectly satisfactory; the soup and meat were especially well cooked. The women and children are happy, have no complaints, and are quite content to stay where they are until they can return to their homes. I shall return to Steytlerville and let everybody know how humane the treatment is. The statement that the women were ragged and barefooted and had to bathe within sight of the military is a shameful falsehood.

On August the 24th General Pole Carew with the Guards' Brigade occupied Belfast, and a few days later Roberts and Buller combined to drive Botha from the last position along the Delagoa Line that he made any serious attempt to defend; and among those taken prisoners by us at Dalmanutha was a German officer, who in due time was sent to Ceylon, and there acquired enough knowledge of English to express in it his views concerning the Boers he served, and the British he opposed. He says among other things that he was wounded five times and received no pay for all his pains. He declares concerning the Boers that—

.... they often ran away from commando and kept quiet, and said to the English that they would not fight any more; but when the district was pacified they took up arms again and looted. They don't know anything about word of honour or oath. They put white flags upon their houses, and fired in the neighbourhood of them. The English were far too lenient at the beginning, and therefore they are now at the opposite extreme.
You should have seen the flourishing Natal, how it was laid waste by the Boers. This looting instinct in them is far stronger than the fighting one. There were also lots of Boers who were praying the whole day instead of fighting; and their officers were perhaps the best prayers and preachers, but certainly the worst fighters; whereas I must

156

confess that the English, although they were headed by very bad generals, very often behaved like good soldiers and finally defeated the greatest difficulties.

The English infantry is splendidly brave and rather skilful; they are good shots too. Tommy Atkins is a wonderful, merry, good-hearted chap, always full of fun and good spirits, and he behaves very kind towards the prisoners. When I was captured, an English colonel who was rather haughty, asked me which English general I thought the best; whereupon I instantly answered 'Tommy Atkins!'

That clever German critic merely put an old long ago discovered truth in new form! "If I blundered," said Wellington, "I could always rely on my soldiers to pull me through." General Pole Carew when, near the close of the war, he was presented with a sword of honour by my native city, Truro, repeated the remark of a distinguished continental soldier attached to his division, who said after seeing British soldiers marching bootless and fighting foodless, he placed the British army "foremost among European armies." So say they all! The German prisoner in Ceylon spoke words of truth and soberness when he said our private soldier is in some respects our best general.

General Tommy Atkins I salute you! You are a credit to your country!

CHAPTER 12

Through Helvetia

On August 24th the tiny little town of Belfast was reached by General Pole Carew's division, including the Guards' Brigade; but though our advent was unopposed, there was heavy fighting on our right, where General Buller, newly arrived from Natal, had the day before approached the immensely strong Boer position at Bergendal. There the Johannesburg police, the most valorous of all the burgher forces, made their last heroic stand three days later, and were so completely wiped out, that Kruger is reported to have been moved to tears when the tidings reached him. It was the last stand the Boer still had nerve enough to make, and after Belfast their continuous retreat quickened into almost a rout. It was on Sunday, the 26th, the Guards moved out to take part in the general assault, and waited for hours behind the shelter of Monument Hill while General French developed his flanking movement on the left. Boer bullets fell freely among us while thus tarrying, and compelled our field hospital to retire further down the slope to a position of comparative safety. Late that afternoon the Guards marched over the brow to face what bade fair to be another serious Sunday battle, yet without any slightest sign of flinching.

"How dear is life to all men," said dying Nelson. It may be so; but these men and their officers from first to last, when duty called, seemed never to count their lives dear unto them. A few casualties, caused by chance bullets, occurred among them before the day closed, but scarcely so much as a solitary Boer was seen by the clearest sighted of them. Once again outflanked, "the brother" once again had fled, and in the deepening darkness we groped our way to our next camping ground.

In our Napoleonic wars the favourite command alike on land and sea was, "Engage the enemy more closely." Each fleet or army kept well in sight of its antagonist, and the fighting was often at such close quarters that musket muzzle touched musket muzzle; but at Belfast Lord Roberts' front was thirty miles in width, and our generals could only guess where their foemen hid by watching for the fire-flash of their long range guns. In offensive warfare the visible contends with the invisible, and it is good generalship that conquers it. At Albuera Soult asserted there was no beating British troops in spite of their generals. But Lord Roberts' generalship seems never to have been at fault, however remote the foe, and thanks thereto Belfast proved to be about the last big fight of the whole campaign.

Early next morning we were vigorously shelled by the still defiant Boers, but from the, for them, fairly safe distance of nearly five miles. Just as the Grenadier officers had finished their breakfast and retired a few yards further afield to get just beyond the reach of those impressive salutations, a shell plumped down precisely where we had been sitting. It made its mark, though fortunately only on the bare bosom of mother earth; but later on in the same day, while we were finishing lunch, another shrapnel burst, almost over our heads, so badly injured a doctor's horse tethered close by that it had to be killed, and compelled another somewhat rapid retirement on our part to the far side of a neighbouring bog. In war time all our feasts are movable!

Before leaving Belfast I called on a German doctor who had been in charge of a Boer military hospital planted in that hamlet, and who told me that for twelve months he had been in the compulsory employ of the Transvaal Government. Commandeered at Johannesburg, he had accompanied the burghers from place to place till he had grown utterly sick of the whole business; and all the more because he had received no payment for his services except in promissory notes—which were worthless. He also stated that over three hundred foreigners had been landed at Delagoa Bay as ambulance men, wearing the red cross armlet; as such they had proceeded to Pretoria for enrolment, and there he had seen every man of them strip off the red cross, shouldering instead the bandolier and rifle. Thus were fighting men and mercenaries smuggled through Portuguese territory to the Boer fighting lines; and in this as in many other ways was that red cross abused. He wastes his time who tries to teach the Boers some new trick. In this war they have amply proved that in that matter they have nought to learn, except the unwisdom of it all, and the sureness of the retribution it involves. Even in battle and battle times clean hands are best.

On leaving the neighbourhood of Belfast we soon found ourselves marching through Helvetia, the Switzerland of South Africa, a region of insurmountable precipices and deep defiles, where scarcely any foliage was found, and in that winter season no verdure. There rose in all directions towering hills, which sometimes bore upon their brow a touch of real majesty; and when crowned, as we saw them, with fleecy mist, resembled not remotely the snow-clad Alps. Indeed, during that whole week the toils and travels of the Guards brought to the mind of many the familiar story of Hannibal and his vast army crossing the Alps; only the Carthaginian general had no heavy guns and long lines of ammunition wagons to add to his already enormous difficulties; his men had little to carry on their broad backs compared with what a modern Guardsman has to shoulder; nor did Hannibal take with him a small army corps of newspaper correspondents to chronicle all the petty disasters and delays met with by the way. Few commanders-in-chief are lovers of correspondents, whether of the professional or of the private type. Tell-tale tongues and pens may perchance do more mischief than machine guns and mausers!

At the latter end of the week our men had to climb over what seemed to be the backbone of that terrific region, with results almost disastrous to our long train of transport wagons. Botha, whose retreat towards Lydenberg our flanking movement had apparently prevented, we failed to find; so after fighting a mild rear-guard action, we scarce knew with whom, we encamped that night for the first and last time side by side with Buller's column.

The major part, however, of the Grenadier battalion remained till next morning far away in the rear to guard our huge convoy while climbing up and climbing down the perilous ridge just referred to, with the result that some of us forming the advanced party found ourselves without food or shelter. Yet the soldierly courtesy which has so often hastened to my help during this campaign did not fail in this new hour of need. A sergeant-major of the bearer company most graciously lent me his own overcoat, the night being bitterly cold; the officers of the Scots Guards not only invited me to dine with them, but one of them supplied me with a rug, whilst another pressed on me the loan of his mackintosh "to keep off the dew," and thus enwrapped I lay once more on the bare ground, well sheltered behind a sheet of corrugated iron, which I fortunately found stuck on end as though put there by some unknown Boer benefactor for my special benefit. In fashion thus lordly were all my wants continually supplied. The wild wind that night blew away a second sheet of iron that another young officer, with almost filial thoughtfulness, placed over me after I had gone to rest, but the original sheet maintained its perpendicular position, and by its welcome protection supplied me with a fresh illustration of the familiar saying, "He stayeth His rough wind in the day of His east wind."

Thus toiling we reached at last a plateau about 5000 feet above sea level, from which we looked down into the famous Waterfall Gorge, a sheer descent of 1000 feet. Down into it there drops from Waterval Boven the cogwheel section of the Delagoa Bay Railway, and in it there nestles a Swiss-like village, with hotel and hospital and railway workshops. As at Abraham's Kraal we captured the President's silk hat but let the President's head escape, so here we captured the President's professional cook, but the day before we arrived the President's private railway car,—his ever-shifting capital,—had eluded our pursuit, together with the President himself and the golden capital, in the shape of abounding coin he carried with him. The tidings proved to us a feast of Tantallus, so near and yet so far! How our men sighed for a sight of that car, and for the fingering of that coin! "At last I have him," said the exulting French General Soult of Wellington, at the battle of St Pierre, but his exultation proved distressingly premature. So did ours! Car and capital vanished just in the nick of time through that Waterfall Gorge, and to this day have never been disgorged.

From even descending into that gorge the whole brigade of Guards was held back for four-and-twenty hours by a solitary invisible sniper, hidden, no one could find out where, in some secure crevice of the opposite cliff. One of our mounted officers riding down to take possession of the village was seriously wounded; and some of the scouts already there were compelled through the same course to keep under close shelter. So the naval guns, the field guns, and the pom-poms were each in turn called to the rescue, and gaily rained shot and shell for hours on every hump and hollow of that opposite cliff, but all in vain; for after each thunderous discharge on our side, there came a responsive "ping" from the valiant mauser-man on the other side. Then the whole battalion of Scots Guards was invited to fire volley after volley in the same delightfully vague fashion, till it seemed as though no pin point or pimple on the far side of the gorge could possibly have failed to receive its own particular bullet; but—

What gave rise to no little surprise,
Nobody seemed one farthing the worse!

Just as the sun set the last sound we heard was the parting *ping* of Brother Invisible. So no man might descend into the depths that night, hotel or no hotel! Even at midnight we were startled out of our sleep by the quite unexpected boom of our big guns, which had, of course during daylight, been trained on a farmhouse lying far back from the precipice opposite to us, and were thus fired in the dead of night under the impression that the sniper, and perhaps his friends, were peacefully slumbering there. If so, the chances are he sniped no more. Next day at noon we began to clamber down to the level of the railway line, and found ourselves in undisturbed possession, after so prolonged and costly a bombardment called forth by a single, stubborn mauser.

Meanwhile the eighteen hundred English prisoners who had so long been kept in durance vile at Nooitgedacht, the next station on the rail to Portuguese Africa, received their unconditional release, with the exception of a few officers, still retained as hostages; and all the afternoon, indeed far on into the night, these men came straggling, now in small groups and now in large, into our expectant and excited camp. They told us of the crowds of disconsolate Boers, some by road, some by rail, who had passed their prison enclosure in precipitate retreat, bearing wagon loads of killed or wounded with them. Among them were men of almost all nationalities, including a few surviving members of the late Johannesburg police, who declared that during that one week they had lost no less than one hundred and fifteen of their own special comrades.

The prisoners also informed us that the Boer officer who dismissed them expressed the belief that in a few days more Boer and Briton would again be friends—an expectation we were slow to share, however eager we might be to see this miracle of miracles actually wrought. In the very midst of the battle of the Baltic, Nelson sent a letter to the Danish Prince Regent, with whom he was then fighting, and addressed it thus: "To the Danes, the Brothers of Englishmen." Within little more than half a century from that date the daughter of the Danish throne became heir to the Queenship of England's throne; and our Laureate rightly voiced the whole nation's feeling when to that fair bride he said:

"We are each all Dane in our welcome of thee."

When Nelson penned that strange address amid the flash and fire of actual battle, it was with the true insight of a seer. The furious foes of his day are the fast friends of ours, and by the end of another half-century a similar transformation may be wrought in the present relationship between Boer and Briton, who are quite as near akin as Dane and Englishman. But to lightly talk of such foes becoming friends "in a few days" is to misread the meaning and measure of a controversy that is more than a century old. Between victors and vanquished, both of so dogged a type, it requires more than a mere treaty of peace to beget goodwill.

Some of these now released prisoners were among the very first to be captured, and so had spent many weary weeks in the Waterval Prison near Pretoria, and were among those who had been decoyed away to these remote and seemingly unassailable mountain fastnesses. They had thus been in bonds altogether ten interminable months. Multiplied hardships had during that period necessarily been theirs, and others for which there was no real need or excuse; but they frankly confessed that as a whole their treatment by the Boers, though leaving much to be desired, had seldom been hard or vindictive.

There were others of these prisoners, however, who were sick or wounded, and therefore were quite unable to climb from the open door of their prison to our lofty camp; so to fetch these I saw seven ambulance wagons made ready to set out with the usual complement of medical orderlies and doctors. These I seriously thought of accompanying on their errand of mercy, but was mercifully hindered. Those red cross wagons we saw no more for ever. The Boers were said to be short of wagons, and asserted that in some way some of our men had done them recent wrong which they wished to avenge. But whatever the supposed provocation or pretext, it was in violation of all the recognised usages of war that those wagons were captured and kept. It was no less an outrage to make prisoners of doctors and orderlies arriving on such an errand. No protests on their part or pleadings for speedy return to duty prevailed. They were compelled to accompany or precede the Boers in their flight to Delagoa Bay, from thence were shipped to Durban, and after long delay rejoined the Brigade on its return to Pretoria. For such highhanded proceedings the Transvaal Government clearly cannot be held responsible, for at that time it had ceased to exist, and more than ever the head of each commando had become a law unto himself. It would be false to say that a fine sense of honour did not anywhere exist in the now defunct Republic, but it is perfectly fair to assert that on the warpath our troops were compelled to tread it was not often found. Yet in every department of life he that contendeth for the mastery is never permanently crowned unless he contend lawfully.

The prettily situated and well appointed hospital at Waterval Onder was originally erected for the use of men employed on the railway, but for months prior to the arrival of the British troops had been in possession of the Boer Government, and was full of sick and wounded burghers, with whom I had many an interesting chat and by whom I was assured that though we might think it strange they still had hope of ultimate success. Among the rest was a German baron, well trained of course, as all Germans are, for war, who on the outbreak of hostilities had consented at Johannesburg to be commandeered, burgher or no burgher, to fight the battles of the Boers, in the justice of whose cause he avowed himself a firm believer. He therefore became an artillery officer in the service of the Transvaal, and while so employed had been badly hit by the British artillery, with the result that his right arm was blown off, his left arm horribly shattered, and two shrapnel bullets planted in his breast. Yet seldom has extreme suffering been borne in more heroic fashion than by him, and he actually told me, in tones of admiration, that the British artillery practice was really *beautiful*. On such a point he should surely be a competent judge seeing that he was himself a professor of the art, and had long stood not behind but in front of our guns, which is precisely where all critics ought to be planted. Their criticisms would then be something worth.

The baron's case was typical of thousands more. Men from all the nations of Europe, and therefore all trained to arms, had been encouraged to settle in various civil employments under the Transvaal Government long before the war began—on the railway, at the dynamite works, in the mines; and so were all ready for the rifle the moment the rifle was ready for them. At once they formed themselves into vigorous commandoes, according to their various nationalities,—Scandinavian, Hollander, French, and German. Even after the war began these foreign commandoes were largely recruited from Europe; French and German steamers landed parties of volunteers for the burgher forces nearly every week at Lorenço Marques. The French steamer *Gironde* brought an unusually large contingent, a motley crowd, including, so it is said, a large proportion of suspicious looking characters. But the most notorious and mischievous of all these queer contingents was the Irish American Brigade. As far back as the day of Marlborough and Blenheim there was an Irish Brigade assisting the French to fight against the English, and with such fiery courage that King George cursed the abominable laws which had robbed him of such excellent fighting material. But at the same time there was about them so much of reckless folly that their departure from the Emerald Isle was laughingly hailed as "The flight of the wild geese." New broods of these same wild geese found their way to the Transvaal, and there made for themselves a name, not as resistless fighters, but as irrestrainable looters. These men linked to the *bywoners*, or squatters, the penniless Dutch of South Africa, did little to help the cause they espoused, but many a time have caused every honest God-fearing burgher to blush by reason of their irrepressible lawlessness.

Among the British patients in this hospital was a magnificent young Australian, who it was feared had been mortally wounded in a small scrimmage round a farmhouse not far away, but who apparently began decidedly to mend from the time the general came to his bedside to say he should be recommended for the distinguished service medal. "That has done me more good than medicine," said he to me a few minutes after. Nevertheless, when ten days later we returned from Koomati Poort, he lay asleep in the little Waterval Cemetery, alas, like Milton's Lycidas, "dead ere his prime."

These Australians being all mounted men, and of an exceptionally fearless type, have suffered in a very marked degree, in just such outpost affairs, by the arts and horrors of sniping. Sportsmen hide from the game they hunt, and bide their time to snipe it. It is in that school the Boer has been trained in his long warfare with savage men and savage beasts. A bayonet at the end of his rifle is to him of no use. He seldom comes to close quarters with hunted men or beasts till the life is well out of them; and so in this war he has shown himself a not too scrupulous sportsman, rather than a soldier, to the undoing of many a scout; and in this fashion, as well as by white flag treachery, the adventurous Australians have distressingly often been victimised. At Manana, four miles east of Lichtenberg, one of their officers, Lieutenant White, was thus treacherously shot while going to answer the white flag displayed by the Boers. He was the pet of the Bushmen's Corps, and concerning him his own men said, "We all loved him, and will avenge him." So round his open grave his comrades solemnly joined hands and pledged themselves never again to recognise the waving of a Boer white flag. My assistant chaplain, with the Bushmen, himself an Australian, emphatically declared that as in the beginning so was it to the end; his men were killed not in fair fight but by murderous sniping. He was with them when Pietersburg was surrendered without a fight, but when they marched through to take possession they were resolutely shot at with explosive bullets from a barricaded house in the centre of the town, till the angry Bushmen broke open the door, and then the sniper sniped no more. On reaching the northern outskirts they again found themselves sniped, they knew not from whence. Several horses were wounded, a trooper was killed on the spot; so was Lieutenant Walters; and Captain Sayles was so badly hit he died two days afterwards. Yet no fighting was going on. The town was undefended, and the Boers in full retreat. This sniper was at last discovered hiding almost close at hand in a big patch of tall African grass. He turned out to be a Hollander schoolmaster, who, finding himself surrounded, sprang upon his knees, threw up his arms and laughingly cried, "All right, khakis, I surrender!" But that was his last laugh; and he lies asleep today in the same cemetery as his three victims.

That cemetery soon after I saw; and in the adjoining camp messed with a group of irregular officers, some of whom ultimately yielded to this spirit of lawless avenging, but were, in consequence, sternly court-marshalled, and suffered the extreme penalty of the law. It is, however, the only case of the kind that has come to my knowledge during thirty months of provocative strife.

Close to the railway station at Waterval Onder was a comfortable little hotel, kept by a French proprietor, whose French cook had deserted him, and who would not therefore undertake to cater for the Grenadier officers, though he courteously placed his dining-room at their disposal, with all that appertained thereto; and sold to them almost his entire stock of drinkables, probably at fancy prices. The men of the Norfolk Regiment are to this day called *Holy Boys* because their forbears in the Peninsular War, so it is said, gave their Bibles for a glass of wine;

but the Norfolks are not the only lovers of high-class liquor the army contains, though army Bibles will not now suffice to buy it. British officers on the trek, however, not only know how to appreciate exquisitely any appropriate home comforts, when for a brief while procurable, but also how to surrender them un-murmuringly at a moment's notice when duty so requires. We had been in possession of our well-appointed hotel table only two days when a sudden order sent us all trekking once again.

It is worth noting that this French hotelkeeper and the Ger-man baron in the adjoining hospital had both fought, though of course on opposite sides, in the great Franco-Prussian war of thir-ty years ago, and now they found themselves overwhelmed by an-other great war wave in one of the remotest and seemingly most inaccessible fastnesses of South Central Africa. In this new war between Boer and Briton the German lost a limb, if not his life, and the Frenchman a large part of his fortune. So intimately are men of all nationalities now bound in the same bundle of life!

On Monday afternoon we marched to Nooitgedacht, where the prisoners already referred to had been confined like sheep in a pen for many a weary week. That pen was made by a double-barbed wire fence; the inner fence consisting of ten strands of wire, about eight inches apart, and the outer fence of five strands, with sundry added entanglements; and a series of powerful elec-tric lights was specially provided to watch and protect the whole vast area thus enclosed. It gave me a violent spasm of heart sick-ness as I thought of English officers and men by hundreds be-ing thus ignominiously hemmed in and worse sheltered than convicts. They had latterly been allowed to erect for themselves grotesquely rough hovels or hutches, many of which they set on fire when suddenly permitted to escape, so that as I found it the whole place looked indescribably dirty and desolate.

Even the shelters provided for the officers, and the hospital hastily erected for the sick, were scarcely fit to stable horses in, and were by official decree doomed to be given to the flames as the surest way of getting rid of the vermin and other vilenesses, of which they contained so rich a store. Here I found huge medicine bottles, never made for the purpose, on which the names of sundry of our sick officers remained written, to wit: *Lieut. Mowbray, one tablespoonful four times a day. 3. VIII. 1900.* In one of these bunks I found a packet of religious leaflets, one of which contained Hart's familiar hymn:

> Come ye weary, heavy laden,
> Lost and ruined by the fall;
> If you tarry till you are better,
> You will never come at all.
> Not the righteous,
> Sinners, Jesus came to call.

Although, therefore, religious services were never held in that prison pen, the men were not left absolutely without religious counsel and consolation. I was unfeignedly glad thus to find in that horrible place medicine for the soul as well as physic for the body, and some of those leaflets I brought away; but the physic I thought it safest not to sample.

Over this unique combination of prison house and hospital there floated a very roughly-made and utterly tattered red cross flag, which now serves as a memento of one of the most humiliating sights it ever fell to my lot to witness, and I could not help picturing to myself the overpowering heartache those prisoners must have felt as hour after hour they were hurried farther and yet farther still through deep defiles and vast mountain fastnesses into a region where it must have seemed as though hope or help could never reach them. But "men, not mountains, determine the fate of nations"; and today, through the mercy of our God, that pestilential pen is no longer any Englishman's prison.

Our next halting place was at Godwand River, still on the Delagoa line, and here we found a wee bit of river scenery almost rivalling the beauty of the stream that has given to Lynmouth its world-wide fame. At this little frequented place two rivers meet, which even in the driest part of the dry season are still real rivers, and would both make superb trout streams, if once properly stocked, as many a river at home has been.

But just a little farther on we found scenery immeasurably more grand than anything we had ever seen before. The Dutch name of this astounding place is Kaapsche Hoop, which seems reminiscent of the *Cape of Good Hope*, though it lies prodigiously far from any sea. It apparently owes its sanguine name to the fact that hereabouts the earliest discoveries of gold in the Transvaal were made. But it is also popularly called the Devil's Kantoor, just as in the Valley of Rocks at Lynton we have the Devil's Cheesering, and other possessions of the same sable owner. This African marvel is, however, much more than a mere valley of rocks, and it bids absolute defiance to my ripest descriptive powers. It is a vast area covered with rocks so grotesquely shaped and utterly fantastic as would have satisfied the artistic taste, and would have yielded fresh inspiration to the soul of a Gustave Doré. The rocks are evidently all igneous and volcanic, but often stand apart in separate columns, and sometimes bear a striking resemblance to enormous beasts or images that might once have served for Oriental idols.

Indeed, looked at by the bewitching but deceptive light of the moon, the whole place lends itself supremely well to every man's individual fancy, and even my unimaginative mind could easily have brought itself to see here a once majestic antediluvian city with its palaces and temples, but now wrecked and ruined by manifold upheavals of nature, and worn into rarest mockeries of its ancient splendours by the wild storms of many a millennium.

What I did certainly see, however, among those rocks were sundry roughly constructed shelters for snipers, who were therefrom to have picked off our men and horses as they crossed the adjacent drift. Terrible havoc might have been wrought in the ranks of the Guards' Brigade, without apparently the loss of a single Transvaaler's life, but there is no citadel under the sun the Boers just then had heart enough to hold.

Immediately adjoining this unique city of rocks is a stupendous cliff from which, our best travelled officers say, the finest panoramic view in the whole world is obtained. The cliff drops almost straight down twelve or fifteen hundred feet, and at its base huge baboons could be seen sporting, quite heedless of an onlooking army. Straight across what looked like an almost level plain, which, nevertheless, was seamed by many a deep defile and scarred by the unfruitful toil of many a gold-seeker, lay another great range of hills, with range rising beyond range, but with the town of Barberton, which I visited twenty months later, lying like a tiny white patch at the foot of the nearest range, some twenty miles away. To the right this plateau looked as though the tempestuous waves of the Atlantic had broken in at that end with overwhelming force, and then had been suddenly arrested and petrified while wave still battled with wave. It is such a view of far-reaching grandeur as I may never hope to see again, even were I to roam the wide world round; and could Kaapsche Hoop, with its absolutely fascinating attractiveness, be transplanted to, say Greenwich Park, any enterprising vendor of tea and shrimps who managed to secure a vested interest in the same, might reasonably hope to make such a fortune out of it as even a Rothschild need not despise.

CHAPTER 13

War's Wanton Waste

Day after day we steadily worked our way *down* to Koomati Poort, even when climbing such terrific hills that we sometimes seemed like men toiling to the top of a seven-storied house in order to reach the cellar. Hence Monday morning found us still seemingly close to "The Devil's Kantoor," which we had reached on the previous Saturday, though meanwhile we had tramped up and down and in and out, till we could travel no farther, all day on Sunday.

During that Sunday tramp there crossed into our lines General Schoeman, driving in a Cape cart drawn by four mules, on his way to Pretoria *via* the Godwand River railway station. Months before he had joined in formally handing over Pretoria to the British, and had been allowed to return to his farm on taking the oath of neutrality. That oath he had refused to break, so he was made a prisoner by his brother Boers. It was in Barberton gaol General French found him and once more set him free. Such a man deemed himself safer in the hands of his foes than of his friends, so was hasting not to his farm but to far-off Pretoria. This favourite commandant was by the Boers called "King David," and not only in the authoritativeness of his tone, but also in the sharp diversities of his martial experiences, bore some not remote resemblance to his ancient namesake.

Far as either of us then was from foreseeing it, the general's path and mine, though just now so divergent, were destined to meet once more. Within a year in Pretoria on the following Whit-Sunday I was sitting in the house of a friend, and was startled, as all present were, by the firing, as we all supposed, of one of our huge 4.7 guns. Later in the day we learned it was the bursting of a 4.7 shell, nearly two miles away from where we heard the dread explosion. That particular British shell happened to be the first that had long ago been fired in the fight near Colesberg, and as it had fallen close to the general's tent without bursting, he brought it away to keep as a curio, and on that particular Sunday, so it is said, was showing it to a Boer friend, and explaining that the new explosive now used by the English is perfectly harmless when properly handled.

His demonstration, however, proved tragically inconclusive. Precisely what happened there is now no one left alive to tell. As in a moment the part of the house in which the experimenters sat was wrecked, and as I next day noted, some neighbouring houses were sorely damaged. The general was blown almost to pieces; one of his daughters who was sitting at the piano was fatally hurt. On the day of the general's funeral the general's friend died from the effect of the injuries received, and three other members of that family circle barely escaped with their lives.

On my first Whit-Tuesday in South Africa I marched with the triumphant Guards into Pretoria. On this second Whit-Tuesday I stood reverently beside the new-made grave of this famous Pretorian general, who had proved himself to be one of the best of the Boers, one of the few concerning whom it is commonly believed that his word was as good as his bond; and thus all strangely a shot ineffectually fired from one of our guns in Cape Colony, claimed eighteen months afterwards this whole group of victims in far-off Pretoria. Thus in the home of peace were so tragically let loose the horrors and havoc of war!

This general's case aptly illustrates one of the most debatable of all points in the conduct of this doubly lamentable struggle. Whilst those who were far away from the scene of operations denounced what they deemed the wanton barbarities of the British, those on the spot denounced almost as warmly what they deemed the foolish and cruel clemency by which the war was so needlessly prolonged. These local complainers asserted that if every surrendered burgher had been compelled to bring in not a rusty sporting rifle, but a good mauser, a good supply of cartridges and a good horse, the Boers would much sooner have reached the end of their resources. That saying is true. Our chiefs assumed they were dealing with only honourable men, and so in this matter let themselves be sorely befooled. Some who surrendered to them one week, were busy shooting at them the next, with rifles that had been buried instead of being given up; and among those who thus proved false to their plighted troth were, alas, ministers of the Dutch Reformed Church.

When near the close of the war I paid a visit to Klerksdorp I was informed by absolutely reliable witnesses that one of the predikants of that neighbourhood had not been required to take an oath because of his sacred calling, and his simple word of honour was accepted. Yet at the time of my visit he was out on commando, harassing with his rifle the very village in which his own wife was still residing under our protection. Next day at Potchetstroom eye-witnesses told me that one of Cronje's chaplains, whom long ago we had set at liberty, soon after seized bandolier and rifle in defiance of all honour, and so a second time became a prisoner. "Straying shepherds, straying sheep!" When pastors thus proved unprincipled, their people might well hold perverted views as to what honour means and oaths involve.

It is further maintained by these protesters against excessive clemency that all surrendered burghers should have been placed in laagers, or sent to the coast on parole, where they could not have been compelled or tempted to take up arms again; but it was this express promise that they should return to their farms there personally to protect families and flocks and furniture, that induced them to come in. They would never have surrendered to be sent far afield, but would have remained in the fighting line to the finish. All was not gained that was hoped for by this generous policy, but it was not such an utter failure as some suppose; and it at least served to pacify public opinion. The experiment of dealing gently with surrendered foemen was fairly tried, and if in part it failed the fault was not ours!

At the latter end, when guerrilla warfare became the order of the day, and the only end aimed at was not fighting, but the mere securing or destruction of food supplies, it became necessary to sweep the *veldt* as with a broom, and to bring within the British lines everybody still left and everybody's belongings; but even then it was a gigantic task, involving much wrecking of what could not be removed; and in the earlier stages of the war such a sweep, if not actually enormously beyond the strength available for it, would certainly have involved many a fatal delay in the progress of the troops.

This championship of clemency is no new thing in the war annals of our island home, and Lord Roberts, in his insistence on it, did but tread in the steps of the very mightiest of his predecessors. Wellington during the Peninsular wars actually dismissed from his service and sent back in disgrace to Spain 25,000 sorely-needed Spanish soldiers, simply because he could not restrain their wayside barbarities. He recognised that a policy which outrages humanity, in the long run means disaster; and frankly confessed concerning his troops, that if they plundered they would ruin all. In a precisely similar vein is Nelson's last prayer, which constitutes the last entry but one in his diary:

> May the great God, whom I worship, grant to my country .... a glorious victory. May no misconduct in anyone tarnish it, and may humanity after victory be the predominant feature in the British fleet.

It was in the spirit of Nelson's prayer and Wellington's precept that Lord Roberts strove to conduct his South African operations. With what success let all the world bear witness!

From *The Three Sisters*, which we reached on our Sabbathless Sunday, we tramped all day on Monday till we reached a tributary of the Crocodile River close to the Noordkaap railway station, about seven miles out from Barberton, which we were not then privileged to visit. Near this place we found the famous Sheba gold mine, its costly machinery for the present lying idle, and its cottages deserted at the stern bidding of intruding war— that most potent disturber of the industries of peace. Here from the loftiest mountain peaks were cables, with cages attached, sloping down to the gold-crushing house; and across the river, in which, crocodiles or no crocodiles, we enjoyed a delicious bathe, there was a similar steel rope suspended as the only possible though perilous way of getting across when the river is in flood. In this as in all other respects, however, a gracious Providence seemed to watch over us for good, seeing that not once during all the eleven months we had been in the country had we found a single river so full as to be unfordable. Moreover, though now tramping through a notorious fever country, the long overdue rain and fever alike lingered in their pursuit of us and overtook us not, so that up to that time not a solitary case of enteric occurred in all our camp. The incessant use of one's heels seems to be the best preservative of health, for it is only among sedentary troops that sickness of any sort really runs riot.

The rations, however, have often been of the short measure type in consequence of the prodigious difficulty of transport over roads that are merely unfrequented tracks, and the utter wearisomeness of such day after day tramps on almost empty stomachs has been so pronounced that the men often laughingly avowed they would prefer fourth class by train to even first class on foot. When they occasionally marched and climbed in almost gloomy silence I sometimes advised them to try the effect on their pedestrian powers of a lively song, and playfully suggested this new version of an old-time melody—

Cheer, boys, cheer,
No more of idle sorrow;
Cheer, boys, cheer,
There'll be another march tomorrow.

But though they readily recognised the appropriateness of the sentiment, they frankly confessed it was impossible to sing on three-quarters of a pound of uncooked flour in place of a full day's rations, which indeed it was. Next day these much-tried men had to wade three times through the river, mostly with their boots and putties on, so that though short of bread and biscuit they were well supplied with "dampers," unfortunately of a sort that soaked but never satisfied.

After passing Joe's Luck, where for us *there was no luck about the house, there was no luck at all*, the Guards reached Avoca, another station on the Barberton branch; and here we found not only a fine railway bridge destroyed with dynamite, but also the railway sheds, recently crammed full with government stores, mostly provisions, now ruthlessly given to the flames and absolutely destroyed. Thousands of tins of condensed milk had flown like bombs in all directions, and like bombs had burst, when the intense heat had turned the confined milk to steam. Butter by the ton had ignominiously ended its days by merely adding so much more fat to the fire. All good things here, laboriously treasured for the benefit of the Transvaal troops, were consumed in quite another fashion from that intended. Even accumulated locomotives to the number of about fifty had been in some cases elaborately mutilated, or caught, and twisted out of all utility, by the devouring flames. So wanton is the waste war begets. The torch has played a comparatively small part in this contest; but it is food supplies that have suffered most from its ravages, and the Boers, with a slimness that baffled us, having thus burned their food, bequeathed to us their famished wives and children. Thousands of these innocents drew full British rations, when thousands of British soldiers were drawing half rations. That is not the Old Testament and Boer-beloved way of waging war, but it foreshadows the slow dawning of an era when, constrained by an overmastering sense of brotherhood—

Men will hang the trumpet in the hall,
And study war no more!

Beyond Avoca we rested for the night at Fever Creek, and were alarmed by the approach of a heavy thunderstorm just as we were commencing our dinner in the dense darkness. So I crept for refuge between the courses of our homely meal under a friendly wagon, and thence came forth from time to time as wind and weather permitted, to renew acquaintance with my deserted platter. Finally, when the storm had somewhat abated, we sought the scanty protection and repose to be found under our damp blankets. That for us with such favouring conditions Fever Creek did not justify its name seems wonderful.

On the Wednesday of that week the Guards' Brigade made a desperate push to reach Kaap Muiden, where the Barberton branch joins the main line to Delagoa Bay, though the ever-haunting transport difficulty made the effort only imperfectly successful. Three out of the four battalions were compelled to bivouac seven miles behind, while the one battalion that did that night reach the junction had at the finish a sort of racing march to get there. While resting for a few minutes outside the Lion's Creek station the colonel told his men that they were to travel the rest of the way by rail; whereupon they gave a ringing cheer and started at a prodigious pace to walk down the line in momentary expectation of meeting the presumably approaching train. Each man seemed to go like a locomotive with full head of steam on, and it took me all my time and strength to keep up with them. Nevertheless that train never met us. It never even started, and at that puffing perspiring pace the battalion proceeded all the way on foot. We had indeed come by *rail*, but that we found was quite another thing from travelling by *train*; and the sequel forcefully reminded one of the simpleton who was beguiled into riding in a sedan-chair from which both seat and bottom had been carefully removed. When the ride was over he is reported to have summed up the situation by saying he might as well have walked but for "the say so" of the thing. And but for the say so of the thing that merrily beguiled battalion might as well have gone by road as by rail.

It was, however, a most wonderful sight that greeted them as they stumbled through the darkness into the junction. At one end of the station there was a huge engine-house, surrounded as well as filled, not only with locomotives but also with gigantic stacks of food stuffs, now all involved in one vast blaze that had not burned itself out when the Brigade returned ten days later. There were long trains of trucks filled with flour, sugar and coffee, over some of which paraffin had been freely poured and set alight. So here a truck and there a truck, with one or two untouched trucks between, was burning furiously. In some cases the mischief had been stopped in mid-career by friendly *Kaffir* hands, which had pulled off from this truck and that a newly-kindled sack, and flung it down between the rails where it lay making a little bonfire that was all its own. Then too broken sacks of unburnt flour lay all about the place looking in the semi-darkness like the Psalmist's "snow in Salmon"; but flour so flavoured and soaked with paraffin that when that night it was served out to be cooked as best it could be by the famished men some of them laughingly asserted it exploded in the process. Oh, was not that a dainty dish to set before such kings! At the far end of the station were ten trucks of coal blazing more vigorously than in any grate, besides yet other trucks filled with government stationery and no one knows what beside. It was an awe-inspiring sight and pitiful in the extreme.

Though too late to save all the treasure stored at this junction, we nevertheless secured an invaluable supply of rolling stock and of certain kinds of provender, so that for a few days we lacked little that was essential except biscuits for the men and forage for the mules. But to prevent if possible further down the line another such holocaust as took place here, our men started at break of day on a forced march towards Koomati Poort.

The line we learned was in fair working order for the next fifteen miles, and for that distance the heavy baggage with men in charge of the same was sent by train. I did not confess to being baggage nor was I in charge thereof, but none the less when my ever courteous and thoughtful colonel urged me to accompany the baggage for those few miles I looked upon his advice in the light of a command, and so accepted my almost only lift of any sort in the long march from the Orange River to Koomati Poort. The full day's march for the men was twenty-five miles through a region that at that season of the year had already become a kind of burning fiery furnace; and the abridging of it for me by at least a half was all the more readily agreed to because my solitary pair of boots was unfortunately in a double sense on its last legs. A merciful man is merciful to his boots, especially when they happen to be his only pair.

Nor in the matter of leather alone were these Guardsmen lamentably lacking. One of the three famous Napier brothers when fighting at close quarters in the battle of Busaco fiercely refused to dismount that he might become a less conspicuous mark for bullets, or even to cover his red uniform with a cloak. "This," said he, "is the uniform of my regiment, and *in it I will show*, or fall this day." Barely a moment after a bullet smashed his jaw.

At the very outset of the Boer war, to the sore annoyance of Boer sharpshooters, the British War Office in this one respect showed great wisdom. All the pomp and pride and circumstance of war were from the outset laid aside, especially in the matter of clothing; but though in that direction almost all regimental distinctions, and distinctions of rank, were deliberately discarded, so that scarcely a speck of martial red was anywhere to be seen, the clothing actually supplied proved astonishingly short-lived. The roughness of the way soon turned it into rags and tatters, and disreputable holes appeared precisely where holes ought not to be. On this very march I was much amused by seeing a smart young Guardsman wearing a sack where his trousers should have been. On each face of the sack was a huge O. Above the O, in bold lettering, appeared the word *oats*, and underneath the O was printed 80 lbs. The proudest man in all the brigade that day seemed he! Well-nigh as travel-stained were we, and torn, as Hereward the Wake when he returned to Bruges.

On Sunday, September 23rd, at Hector Spruit we most unexpectedly lingered till after noonday, partly to avoid the intense heat on our next march of nineteen miles through an absolutely waterless wilderness, and partly because of the enormous difficulties involved in finding tracks or making them through patches of thorny jungle. We were thus able to arrange for a surprise parade service, and when that was over some of our men who had gone for a bathe found awaiting them a still more pleasant surprise. In the broad waters of the Crocodile they alighted on a large quantity of abandoned and broken Boer guns and rifles. Such abandonment now became an almost daily occurrence, and continued to be for more than another six months, till all men marvelled whence came the seemingly inexhaustible supply. At Lydenberg, which Buller captured on September 6th, and again at Spitzkop which he entered on September 15th, stores of almost every kind were found well-nigh enough to feed and furnish a little army; though in their retreat to the latter stronghold the burghers had flung some of their big guns and no less than thirteen ammunition wagons over the cliffs to prevent them falling into the hands of the British. Never was a nation so armed to the teeth. As nature had made every hill a fortress, so the Transvaal Government had made pretty nearly every hamlet an arsenal; and about this same time French on the 14th, at Barberton, had found in addition to more warlike stores forty locomotives which our foes were fortunately too frightened to linger long enough to destroy. Those locos were worth to us more than a king's ransom!

That afternoon we marched till dark, then lighted our fires, and bemoaned the emptiness of our water bottles, while awaiting the arrival of our blanket wagons. But in half an hour came another sharp surprise, for without a moment's warning we were ordered to resume our march for five miles more. So through the darkness we stumbled as best we could along the damaged railway line. About midnight in the midst of a prickly jungle, a bit of bread and cheese, a drink of water if we had any left, and a blanket, paved the way for brief repose; but at four o'clock next morning we were all astir once more, to find ourselves within sight of a tiny railway station called Tin Vosch, where two more locomotives and a long line of trucks awaited capture.

On Monday, September 24th, at about eight o'clock in the morning, to General Pole Carew and Brigadier-General Jones fell the honour of leading their Guardsmen into Koomati Poort, the extreme eastern limit of the Transvaal—and that without seeing a solitary Boer or having to fire a single bullet. The French historian of the Peninsular War declares that "the English were the best marksmen in Europe—indeed the only troops who were perfectly practised in the use of small arms." But then their withering volleys were sometimes fired at a distance of only a few yards from the wavering masses of their foes, and under such conditions good marksmanship is easy to attain. A blind man might bet he would not miss. On the other hand, he must be a good shot indeed who can hit a foe he never sees. In these last weeks there were few casualties among the Boers, because they kept well out of casualty range. They were so frightened they even forgot to snipe. The valiant old President so long ago as

September 11th had fled with his splendidly well-filled money bags across the Portuguese frontier; abandoning his burghers who were still in the field to whatever might chance to be their fate. That fate he watched, and waited for, from the secure retreat of the Portuguese Governor's veranda close by the Eastern Sea, where he sat and mused as aforetime on his *stoep* at Pretoria; his well-thumbed Bible still by his side, his well-used pipe still between his lips. Surely Napoleon the Third at Chislehurst, broken in health, broken in heart, was a scarcely more pathetic spectacle! Six or seven days later the old man saw special trains beginning to arrive, all crowded with mercenary fighting men from many lands, all bent only on following his own uncourageous example, seeking personal safety by the sea. First came 700; then on the 24th, the very day the Guards entered Koomati Poort, 2000 more, who were mostly ruined burghers, and who thus arrived at Delagoa Bay to become like Kruger himself the guests or prisoners of the Portuguese.

To the Portuguese we ourselves owe no small debt of gratitude, for they had sternly forbidden the destruction of the magnificent railway bridge across the Koomati, in which their government held large financial interests. But other destruction they could not hinder.

Just in front of us lay the superbly lovely junction of the Crocodile with the Koomati River, and appropriately enough I then saw in midstream, clinging to a rock, a real crocodile, though, like the two Boer Republics, as dead as a door nail. Immediately beyond ran a ridge of hills which served as the boundary between the Transvaal and the Portuguese territory. Along that ridge floated a line of Portuguese flags, and within just a few yards of them the ever-slim Boer had planted some of his long-range guns, not that there he might make his last valiant stand, but that from thence he might present our approaching troops with a few parting shots. This final outrage on their own flag our friendly neighbours forbade. So we discovered the guns still in position but destroyed with dynamite. Thus finding not a solitary soul left to dispute possession with us we somewhat prematurely concluded that at last, through God's mercy, our toils were ended, our warfare accomplished. What wonder therefore if in that hour of bloodless triumph there were some whose hearts exclaimed, "We praise Thee O God, we acknowledge Thee to be the Lord!" To the God of Battles the Boer had made his mutely stern appeal and with this result.

The *Household Brigade Magazine* tells an amusing story of a Guardsman hailing from Ireland who at one of our base hospitals was supplied with some wine as a most welcome "medical comfort." Therein right loyally he drank the Queen's health, and then after a pause startled his comrades by adding, "Here's to old Kruger! God bless him!" Such a disloyal sentiment, so soon tripping up the heels of his own loyalty, called forth loud and angry protests, whereupon he exclaimed, "Why not? Only for him where would the war be? And only for him I would never have sent my old mother the Queen's chocolate!"

The Queen's chocolate is not the only bit of compensating sweetness begotten out of the bitterness of this war. The fiery hostility of Kruger, like the quenchless hate of Napoleon a hundred years ago, has not been without beneficent influence on our national character and destiny, and these two years of war have seemingly done more for the consolidation of the empire than twenty years of peace. Whether he and Steyn used the Africander Bond as their tool or were themselves its tools the outcome of the war is the same. To Great Britain it has so bound Greater Britain in love-bonds and mutual loyalty as to make all the world wonder.

The President of the Transvaal months after the war began is reported to have said: "If the moon is inhabited I cannot understand why John Bull has not yet annexed it"; but with respect to his own beloved Republic he reckoned it was far safer than the moon, for he added: "So surely as there is a God of righteousness, so surely will the Vierkleur be victorious."

What that victory, however, would inevitably have involved was made abundantly plain in the pages of *De Patriot*, the once official organ of the Africander Bond. There, as long ago as 1882, it was written:

The English Government keep talking of a Confederation under the British flag. That will never happen. There is just one hindrance to Confederation, and that is the British flag. Let them take that away, and within a year the Confederation under the Free Africander flag would be established; but so long as the English flag remains here the Africander Bond must be our Confederation. The British must just have Simon's Bay as a naval and military station on the road to India, and give over all Africa to the Africanders. Let every Africander in this Colony (that is, the Cape) for the sake of security take care that he has a good rifle and a box of cartridges, and that he knows how to use them.

English trade is to be boycotted, nor is this veiled hostility to end even there.

Sell no land to Englishmen! We especially say this to our Transvaal brethren. The Boers are the landowners, and the proud little Englishmen are dependent on the Boers. Now that the war against the English Government is over, the war against the English language must begin. It must be considered a disgrace to speak English. The English governess is a pest. Africander parents, banish this pest from your houses!

Now, however, that Kruger is gone, and the Africander Bond has well nigh given up the ghost, English governesses in South Africa will be given another chance, which is at least some small compensation for all the cost and complicated consequences of this wanton war.

Martinus Theunis Steyn, late President of what was once the Orange Free State, is in almost all respects a marked contrast to the Transvaal President, whose folly he abetted and whose flight for a while he shared. Steyn, speaking broadly, is almost young enough to be Kruger's grandson, and was never, as Kruger was from his birth, a British subject, for he was born at Wynburg some few years after the Orange Free State received its independence. Whilst Kruger was never for a single hour under the schoolmaster's rod, and is laughingly said even now to be unable to read anything which he has not first committed to memory, Steyn is a man of considerable culture, having been trained in England as a barrister, and having practised at the bar in Bloemfontein for six years before he became President. He therefore could not plead ignorance as his excuse when he flung his ultimatum in the face of Great Britain and Ireland. Whilst Kruger was a man of war from his youth, a "strong, unscrupulous, grim, determined man," Steyn never saw a shot fired in his life except in sport till this war began, yet all strangely it was the fighting President who fled from the face of the Guards, with all their multitudinous comrades in arms, and never rested till the sea removed him beyond their reach, while the lawyerly President, the man of peace, doubled back on his pursuers, returned by rugged by-paths to the land he had ruined, and there in association with De Wet became even more a fugitive than ancient Cain or the men of Adullam's cave.

That many of his own people hotly disapproved of the course their infatuated ruler took is common knowledge; but by no one has that fact been more powerfully emphasised than by Paul Botha in his famous book *From Boer to Boer*. Rightly or wrongly, this is what, briefly put, Botha says:

> When as a Free Stater I think of the war and realise that we have lost the independence of our little state, I feel that I could curse Martinus Theunis Steyn who used his country as a stepping stone for the furtherance of his own private ends. He sold his country to the Transvaal in the hope that Paul Kruger's mantle would fall on him. The first time Kruger visited the Orange Free State after Steyn's election the latter introduced him at a public banquet with these words, "This is my Father!"
> The thought occurred to me at the time, "Yes, and you are waiting for your father's shoes."
> He hoped to succeed *his father* as President of the combined republics of united South Africa. For this giddy vision he ignored the real interests of our little state, and dragged the country into an absolutely unnecessary and insane war. I maintain there were only two courses open to England in answer to Kruger's challenging policy—to fight, or to retire from South Africa—and it was only possible for men suffering from tremendously swollen heads, such as our leaders were suffering from, to doubt the issue.

I ask any man to tell me what quarrel we had with England? Was any injury done to us? Such questions make one's hair stand on end. Whether knave or fool, Steyn did not prepare himself adequately for his gigantic undertaking. He commenced this war with a firm trust in God and the most gross negligence. But it is impossible to reason with the men now at the front. With the exception of a few officials these men consist of ignorant *bywoners*, augmented by desperate men from the Cape who have nothing to lose, and who lead a jolly rollicking life on commando, stealing and looting from the farmers who have surrendered, and whom they opprobriously call *handsuppers*!

These *bywoners* believe any preposterous story their leaders tell them in order to keep them together. One of my sons who was taken prisoner by Theron because he had laid down his arms, told me, after his escape, it was common laager talk that 60,000 Russians, Americans and Frenchmen were on the water, and expected daily; that China had invaded and occupied England, and that only a small corner of that country still resisted. These are the men who are terrifying their own people. I could instance hundreds of cases to show their atrocious conduct. Notorious thieves and cowards are allowed to clear isolated farmhouses of every valuable. Widows whose husbands have been killed on commando are not safe from their depredations. They have even set fire to dwelling-houses while the inmates were asleep inside.

As to the perfect accuracy of these accusations I can scarcely claim to be a judge, though apparently reliable confirmation of the same reached me from many sources; but I do confidently assert that no kindred accusations can be justly hurled at the men by whose side I tramped from Orange River to Koomati Poort. Their good conduct was only surpassed by their courage, and of them may be generally asserted what Maitland said to the heroic defenders of Hougoumont—"Every man of you deserves promotion."

CHAPTER 14

From Portuguese Africa to Pretoria

Towards sundown on Tuesday, September 24th, while most of the Guards' Brigade was busy bathing in the delicious waters of the Koomati at its juncture with the Crocodile River, I walked along the railway line to take stock of the damage done to the rolling stock, and to the endlessly varied goods with which long lines of trucks had recently been filled. It was an absolutely appalling sight!

Long before, at the very beginning of the war, the Boers, as we have often been reminded, promised to stagger humanity, and during this period of the strife they came strangely near to fulfilling their purpose. They staggered us most of all by letting slip so many opportunities for staggering us indeed. Day after day we marched through a country superbly fitted for defence, a country where one might check a thousand and two make ten thousand look about them. Our last long march was through an absolutely waterless and apparently pathless bush. Yet there was none to say us nay! From Waterval Onder onwards to Koomati Poort not a solitary sniper ventured to molest us. A more complete collapse of a nation's valour has seldom been seen. On September 17th, precisely a week before we arrived at Koomati, special trains crowded with fugitive burghers rushed across the frontier, whence not a few fled to the land of their nativity—to France, to Germany, to Russia—and amid the curious collection of things strewing the railway line, close to the

Portuguese frontier, I saw an excellent enamelled fold-up bed-stead, on which was painted the owner's name and address in clear Russian characters, as also in plain English, thus: *P. Dutil. St. Petersburg, Russie.*

That beautiful little bedstead thus flung away had a tale of its own to tell, and silently assented to the sad truth that this war, though in no sense a war with Russia, was yet a war with Russians and with men of almost every nationality under heaven.

Humanity was scarcely less severely staggered by the lavish destruction of food stuffs and rolling stock we were that day compelled to witness. In the sidings of the Koomati railway station, as at Kaap Muiden, I found not less than half a mile of loaded trucks all blazing furiously. The goods shed was also in flames, and so was a gigantic heap of coals for locomotive use, which was still smouldering months afterwards. Along the Selati branch I saw what I was told amounted to over five miles of empty trucks that had fortunately escaped destruction, and later on proved to us of prodigious use.

A war correspondent, who had been with the Portuguese for weeks awaiting our advent, assured me that the Boers were so dismayed by the tidings of our approach that at first they precipitately fled leaving everything untouched; but finding we apparently delayed for a few hours our coming, they ventured across the great railway bridge in a red cross ambulance train, on which they felt certain we should not fire even if our scouts were already in possession of the place; and so from the shelter of the red cross these firebrands stepped forth to perform their task of almost immeasurable destruction. It is however only fair to add that the great majority of these mischief-makers were declared to be not genuine Boers, but mercenaries,—a much-mixed multitude whose ignominious departure from the Transvaal will minister much to its future wholesomeness and honesty.

Next morning while with several officers I was enjoying a before breakfast bathe, a cry of alarm was raised, and presently I saw those who had hurried out of the water taking careful aim at a crocodile clinging to a rock in midstream. Revolver shot after revolver shot was fired, but I quickly perceived it was the very same crocodile I had seen at that very same spot the day before; and as it was quite dead then I concluded it was probably still dead, though the officers thus furiously assailing it had not yet discovered the fact; so leaving them to continue their revolver practice I quietly returned to the bubbling waters and finished my bathe in peace.

Later on a continuous rifle fire at the river side close to the Guards' camp attracted general attention, and on going to see what it all meant I found a group of Colonials had thus been popping for hours at a huge hippopotamus hiding in a deep pool close to the opposite bank. Every time the poor brute put its nose above the surface of the water half a dozen bullets splashed all around it though apparently without effect. The Grenadier officers pronounced such proceedings cruel and cowardly, but were without authority to put a stop to it. The crocodile is deemed lawful sport because it endangers life, but the Hippo. Transvaal law protects, because it rarely does harm, and is growing rarer year by year. I ventured therefore to tell these Colonials that their sportsmanship was as bad as their marksmanship, and that the pleasure which springs from inflicting profitless pain was an unsoldierly pursuit; but I preached to deaf ears, and when soon after our camp was broken up that Hippo. was still their target.

On the second day of our brief stay at Koomati Poort, I crossed the splendid seven spanned bridge over the Koomati River, and noticed that the far end was guarded by triple lines of barbed wire, nor was other evidence lacking that the Boers purposed to give us a parting blizzard under the very shadow of the Portuguese frontier flags.

Then came a sight not often surpassed since Napoleon's flight from Moscow. Right up to the Portuguese frontier the slopes of the railway line were strewn with every imaginable and unimaginable form of loot and wreckage, flung out of the trains as they flew along by the frightened burghers. Telegraph instruments, crutches, and rocking chairs, frying pans and packets of medicinal powders, wash-hand basins and tins of Danish butter lay there in wild profusion; likewise a homely wooden box that looked up at me and said "Eat Quaker Oats."

At one point I found a great pile of rifles over which paraffin had been freely poured and then set on fire. Hundreds more, broken and scattered, were flung in all directions. Then, too, I saw cases of dynamite, live shells of every sort and size, and piles of boxes on which was painted—

Explosive **Safety Cartridges**
Supplied by Vickers, Maxim & Co.
For the use of the Government of the
South African Republic

Likewise boxes of ammunition, broken and unbroken bearing the brand of *Kynoch Brothers, Birmingham* were there in piles; and it was while some men of the Gordons were superintending the destruction of this ammunition that a terrific explosion occurred a few days later by which three of them were killed and twenty-one wounded, including the *curio* of the regiment, who was stuck all over with splinters like pins in a cushion; and in spite of seven-and-twenty wounds had the daring to survive. Byron somewhere tells of an eagle pierced by an arrow winged with a feather from its own breast, and in this war many a British hero has been riddled by bullets that British hands have fashioned. Moreover, among these bullets that thus littered that railway track I found vast quantities of the soft-nosed and slit varieties of which I brought away some samples; and others coated with a something green as verdigris. It is said that in love and war all is fair; but we should have more readily believed in the much belauded piety of the Boers, if it had deigned to dispense with *soft noses* and *explosive safeties*, which were none the less cruel or unlawful because of British make!

Whole stacks of sugar I also found, in flaming haste to turn themselves into rippling lakes of decidedly overdone toffee; and in similar fashion piled up sacks of coffee berries were roasting themselves not wisely but too well. Pyramids of flour were much in the same way baking themselves into cakes, monstrously misshapen, and much more badly burnt than King Alfred's ever were. "The Boers are poor cooks," laughingly explained our men; "they bake in bulk without proper mixing." Nevertheless, along that line everything seemed very much mixed indeed.

On reaching the Portuguese frontier I somewhat ceremoniously saluted the Portuguese flag, to the evident satisfaction of the Portuguese marines who mounted guard beside it. There were just then about 600 of them on duty at Resina Garcia, and as they were for the most part dressed in spotless white they looked delightsomely clean and cool. Indeed, the contrast between their uniforms and ours was almost painfully acute; but it was the contrast between men of war's men in holiday attire, which no war had ever touched, and weary war-men tattered and torn by ten months' constant contact with its roughest usage. A shameful looking lot we were—but ashamed we were not!

As these foreigners on frontier guard knew not a word of English, and I unfortunately knew not a word of Portuguese, there seemed small chance of any very luminous conversation; but presently I pronounced the magic word "Padre," and pointed to the cross upon my collar, when lo! a look of intelligence crept into the very dullest face. They passed on the word in approving tones from one to another, and I was instantly supplied with quite a new illustration of the ancient legend, *In hoc signo vinces*. In token of respect for my chaplain's badge, without passport or payment, I was at once courteously allowed to cross the line and set foot in Portuguese Africa. There are compensations in every lot, even in a parson's!

The village immediately beyond the frontier is little else than a block or two of solidly built barracks, and a well appointed railway station, with its inevitable refreshment room, in which a group of officers representing the two nationalities were enjoying a friendly lunch. But great was my surprise on discovering that the vivacious Portuguese proprietor presiding behind the bar was a veritable Scotchman hailing from queenly Edinburgh; and still greater was my surprise on hearing a sweetly familiar accent on the lips of a Colonial scout hungrily waiting on the platform outside till the aforesaid officers' lunch was over, and he, a private, might be permitted to purchase an equally satisfying lunch and eat it in that same refreshment room. It was the accent of the far away West Country, and told me its owner was like myself a Cornishman. Yet what need to be surprised? Were I to take the wings of the morning and fly to the uttermost parts of the earth, I should probably find there as at Resina Garcia, thriving Scotchman in possession, and a famished Cornishman waiting at his gate. To these two, in this fashion, have been apportioned the outposts of the habitable globe!

It was to everybody's extreme surprise and delight that at noon on Thursday we received sudden orders to leave Koomati Poort at once, and to leave it not on foot but by rail. The huge baboon, therefore, which had become our latest regimental pet and terror, was promptly transferred to other custody, and our scanty kits were packed with utmost speed. We soon discovered, however, that it was one thing to reach the appointed railway station, and quite another to find the appointed train. Two locomotives, in apparently sound condition, had been selected from among a multitude of utterly wrecked and ruined ones, but serviceable trucks had also to be warily chosen from among the leavings of a vast devouring fire; then the loading of these trucks with the various belongings of the battalion began, and long before that task was finished darkness set in, so compelling the postponement of all journeying till morning light appeared. It was on the King of Portugal's birthday that morning light dawned, and it was to the sound of a royal salute in honour of that anniversary we attempted to start on our westward way, while the troops left behind us joined with those of Portugal in a royal review.

As all the regular railway employees had fled with the departing Boers, it became necessary to call for volunteers from among the soldiers to do duty as drivers, stokers and guards. The result was at times amusing, and at times alarming. Our locomotives were so unskilfully handled that they at once degenerated into the merest donkey engines, and played upon us donkey tricks. One of these amateur drivers early in the journey discovered that he had forgotten to take on board an adequate supply of coal, and so ran his engine back to get it, while we patiently awaited his return. Soon after we made our second start it was discovered that something had gone wrong with the injectors. "The water was

BOER FAMILIES ON THEIR WAY TO A CONCENTRATION CAMP

too hot," we were told, which to us was a quite incomprehensible fault; the water tank was full of steam, and we were in danger of a general blow up. So the fire had to be raked out, and the engine allowed to cool, which it took an unconscionably long time in doing, and we accounted ourselves fortunate in that on a journey so diversified we escaped the further complications that might have been created for us by our ever invisible foes, who managed to wreck the train immediately following ours—so inflicting fatal or other injuries on Guardsmen not a few.

Meanwhile we noted that "fever" trees, with stems of a peculiarly green and bilious hue, abounded on both sides the line; trees so called, not because they produce fever, but because their presence infallibly indicates an area in which fever habitually prevails. Hundreds of the troops that followed us into the fatal valley were speedily fever-stricken, and it is with a sense of devoutest gratitude I record the fact that the Guards' Brigade not only entered Koomati Port without the loss of a single life by bullets, but also left it without the loss of a single life by fever.

At first at the foot of every incline we were compelled to pause while our engines, one in front and one behind, got up an ampler pressure of steam, but presently it was suggested that the hundreds of Guardsmen on board the train should tumble out of the trucks and shove, which accordingly they did, the Colonel himself assenting and assisting. So sometimes shoving, always steaming, we pursued our shining way, as we fondly supposed, towards Hyde Park corner and "Home, sweet Home."

At Waterval Onder we stayed the night, and I was thus enabled to visit once again the tiny international cemetery, referred to in a former chapter, where I had laid to rest an unnamed, because unrecognised, private of the Devons. Now close beside him in that silent land lay the superbly-built Australian, whom I had so often visited in the adjoining hospital, and whom our general had promised to recommend for the Distinguished Service Medal. Not yet eighteen, his life work was early finished; but by heroisms such as his has our vast South African domain been bought; and by graves such as his are the far sundered parts of our world-wide empire knit together.

Throughout this whole journey I was painfully impressed not only by the almost total absence of all signs of present-day cultivation, even where such cultivation could not but prove richly remunerative, but also by the still sadder fact that many of the farmhouses we sighted were in ruins. Along this Delagoa line, as in other parts of the Transvaal, there had been so much sniping at trains, and so many cases of scouts being fired at from farmhouses over which the white flag floated, that this particular form of retribution and repression, which we none the less deplored, seemed essential to the safety of all under our protection; and in defence thereof I heard quoted, as peculiarly appropriate to the Boer temperament and tactics, the familiar lines:

Softly, gently, touch a nettle,
And it stings you for your pains;
Grasp it like a man of mettle,
And it soft as silk remains.

Amajuba led to a fatal misjudgement of the British by the Boer. In all leniency, the latter now recognises only an encouraging lack of grit, which persuades him to prolong the contest by whatever tactics suit him best. Its effect resembles that of the Danegeld our Saxon fathers paid their overseas invaders, with a view to staying all further strife. Their gifts were interpreted as a sign of craven fear, and merely taught the recipients to clamour greedily for more. Long before this cruel war closed it became clear as noonday that Boer hostilities could not be bought off by a crippling clemency, and that an ever-discriminating severity is, in practice, mercy of the truest and most effective type.

How great the pressure on the military authorities became in consequence of these frequent breakages of the railway line, and how serious the inconvenience to the mercantile community, as indeed to the whole civil population, may be judged from the fact that only on the day of my return from Resina Garcia did the Pretoria merchants receive their first small consignments of food stuffs since the arrival of the British troops some four months before. Clothing, boots, indeed goods of any other type than food, they had still not the faintest hope of getting up from the coast for many a week to come. War is always hard alike on public stores and private cupboards; but seldom have the supplies of any town, not actually undergoing a siege, been more nearly exhausted than were those of Pretoria at the time now referred to. For hungry and impecunious folk the City of Roses was fast becoming a bed of thorns.

From Pretoria I accompanied the Guards on what we all deemed our homeward way as far as Norval's Pont. Then the Brigade, as such, was broken up for blockhouse or other widely dispersing duties; and I was accordingly recalled to headquarters for garrison work. At this point, therefore, I must say farewell to the Guard's Brigade.

For over twelve months my association with them was almost absolutely uninterrupted. At meals and on the march, in the comparative quiet of camp life, and on the field of fatal conflict, I was with them night and day; ever receiving from them courtesies and practical kindnesses immeasurably beyond what so entire a stranger was entitled to expect. Officers and men alike made me royally welcome, and won in almost all respects my warmest admiration.

Their unfailing consideration for *the cloth* by no means implied that they were all God-fearing men; nor did many among them claim to be such; but gentlemen were they one and all, whose worst fault was their traditional tendency towards needlessly strong language. To Mr Burgess, the chaplain of the 19th Hussars once said, "The officers of our battalion are a very gentlemanly lot of fellows, and you never hear any of them swear. The colonel is very severe on those who use bad language, and if he hears any he says, 'I tell you I will not allow it. If you want to use such language go out on to the *veldt* and swear at the stones, but I will not permit you to contaminate the men by such language in the lines. I won't have it!'"

Not all battalions in the British army are built that way, nor do all British officers row in the same boat with that aforesaid colonel. Nevertheless, I am prepared to echo the opinion expressed by Julian Ralph concerning the officers with whom he fraternized:—"They were emphatically the best of Englishmen," said he; "well informed, proud, polished, polite, considerate, and abounding with animal health and spirits." As a whole that assertion is largely true as applied to those with whom it was my privilege to associate. Most of them had been educated at one or other of our great public schools, many of them represented families of historic and world-wide renown. It was, therefore, somewhat of an astonishment to see such men continually roughing it in a fashion that navvies would scarcely consent to do at home; drinking water that, as our colonel said, one would not willingly give to a dog; and sometimes sleeping in ditches without even a rug to cover them.

Wild assertions have been made in some ill-informed papers about these officers being ill-informed, and even Conan Doyle complains that he saw only one young officer studying an Army Text-Book in the course of the whole campaign; but then, when kits are cut down to a maximum weight of thirty-seven pounds, what room is there for books even on tactics? The tactics of actual battle are better teachers than any text-books; and a cool head, with a courageous heart, is often of more value in a tight corner than any amount of merely technical knowledge. It is true that some of our officers have blundered, but then, in most cases, it was their first experience of real war, especially of war amid conditions entirely novel. It was more personal initiative, not more text-book; more caution, not more courage that was most commonly required. To inspire his men with tranquil confidence, one officer after another exposed himself to needless perils, and was, as we fear, wastefully done to death. But be that as it may the Guards' Brigade, men and officers alike, I rank among the bravest of the brave; and my association with them for so long a season, I reckon one of the highest honours of a happy life.

CHAPTER 15

A War of Ceaseless Surprises

What Conan Doyle rightly described as "The great *Boer* War" came eventually to be called yet more correctly "The great *Bore* War." It grew into a weariness that might well have worn out the patience and exhausted the resources of almost any nation. No one for a moment imagined when we reached Koomati Poort that we had come only to the half-way house of our toils and travels, and that there still lay ahead of us another twelve months' cruel task. From the very first to the very finish it has been a war of sharp surprises, and to most the sharpest surprise of all has been this its wasteful and wanton prolonging.

We wondered early, and we wondered late, at the seeming exhaustlessness of the Boer resources. In their frequent flights they destroyed, or left for us to capture, almost fabulously large supplies of food and ammunition; yet at the end of two years of such incessant waste *Kaffirs* were still busy pointing out to us remote caves filled with food stuffs, as in Seccicuni's country, or large pits loaded to the brim with cases of cartridges. A specially influential Boer prisoner told me he himself had been present at many such burials, when 250 cases of mauser ammunition were thus secreted in one place, and then a similar quantity in another, and I have it on the most absolute authority possible that when the war began the Boers possessed not less than 70,000,000 rounds of ball cartridge, and 200,000 rifles of various patterns, which would be tantamount to two for every adult Dutchman in all South Africa. Kruger, in declaring war, did not leap before he looked, or put the kettle on the fire without first procuring an ample supply of coal to keep it boiling. For many a month before hostilities commenced, if not for years, all South Africa lay in the hollow of Kruger's hand, excepting only the seaport towns commanded by our naval guns. At any moment he could have overrun our South African colonies and none could have said him nay. These colonies we held, though we knew it not, on Boer sufferance. At the end of two years of incessant fighting we barely made an end of the invasion of Cape Colony and Natal, and the altogether unsuspected difficulty of the task is the true index of the deadliness of the peril from which this dreadful war has delivered the whole empire.

How it was the Boers did not succeed at the very outset in driving the British into the sea, when we had only skeleton forces to oppose them, was best explained to me by a son of the late State Secretary, who penned the ultimatum, and whom I found among our prisoners in Pretoria. The Boers are not farmers. Speaking broadly there is scarcely an acre of ploughed land in all the Transvaal. "The men are shepherds, their trade hath been to feed cattle." But before they could thus, like the Patriarchs, become herdsmen, they perforce still, like their much loved Hebrew prototypes, had to become hunters, and clear the land of savage beasts and savage men. The hunter's instincts, the hunter's tactics were theirs, and no hunter comes out into the open if he can help it. It is no branch of his business to make a display of his courage and to court death. His part is to kill, so silently, so secretly, as to avoid being killed. Traps and tricking, not to say treachery, and shooting from behind absolutely safe cover, are the essential points in a hunter's tactics. Caution to him is more than courage, and it is precisely along those lines the Boers make war. In almost every case when they ventured into the open it was the doing of their despised foreign auxiliaries. The kind of courage required for the actual conquest of the colonies the Boers had never cultivated or acquired. The men who in six months and six days could not rush little Mafeking hoped in vain to capture Cape Town, unless they caught it napping. But in defensive warfare, in cunningly setting snares like that at Sanna's Post, in skilful concealment as at Modder River, when all day long most of our men were quite unable to discover on which side of the stream the Boer entrenchments were, and in what they called clever trickery, but we called treachery, they are absolutely unsurpassable. So was it through the earlier stages of the campaign. So was it through the later stages.

Another cause of Boer failure as explained to me by the State Secretary's son was the inexperience and incompetency of their generals, who had won what little renown was theirs in Zulu or *Kaffir* wars. Amajuba, at which only about half a battalion of our troops took part, was the biggest battle they had ever fought against the British, and it led the more illiterate among them to believe they could whip all England's armies as easily as they could *sjambok* a *Kaffir*. Their leaders of course knew better, but even they believed there was being played a game of bluff on both sides, with this vital difference, however—we bluffed, and, as they full well knew, did not prepare; they bluffed, and, to an extent we never knew, did prepare. Though therefore their generals were amateurs in the arts of modern warfare as so many of our own proved to be, they confidently reckoned that, if they could strike a staggering blow whilst we were as yet unready, they would inevitably win a second Amajuba. Magnanimity would again leave them masters of the situation, and if not, European intervention would presently compel us to arbitrate away our claims. But Joubert's softness, Schoeman's incompetency and Cronje's surrender spoiled the project just when success seemed in sight. One other cause of Boer failure which remained in force to the very last was their utter lack of discipline. My specially frank and intelligent informant said no Boer ever took part in a fight unless he felt so inclined. He claimed liberty to ignore the most urgent commands of his field cornet, and might even unreproved slap him in the face. Such decidedly independent fighting may serve for the defence of an almost inaccessible *kopje*, but an attack conducted on such lines is almost sure to fall to pieces. It was therefore seldom attempted, but many a lawless deed was done, like firing on ambulances and funeral parties, for which no leader can well be held responsible.

This light formation lent itself, however, excellently well to the success of the guerrilla type of warfare, which the Boers maintained for more than twelve months after all their principal towns were taken. Solitary snipers were thus able from safe distances to pick off unsuspecting man, or horse, or ox, and, if in danger of being traced, could hide the bandolier and pose as a peace-loving citizen seeking his own lost ox.

In some cases small detachments of our men on convoy or outpost duty were cut off by these ever-watchful, ever-wandering bands of Boers, and an occasional gun or pom-pom was temporarily captured, a result for which in one case at least extra rum rations were reputed to be responsible. But it must be remembered that our men and officers, regular and irregular alike, were as inexperienced as the Boers in many of the novel duties this war devolved upon them; that the Transvaal lends itself as scarcely any other country under the sun could do to just such surprises, and that the ablest generals served by the trustiest scouts have in the most heroic periods of our history sometimes found themselves face to face with the unforeseen. We are assured, for instance, that even on the eve of Waterloo both Blucher and Wellington were caught off their guard by their great antagonist. On June 15th, at the very moment when the French columns were actually crossing the Belgian frontier, Wellington wrote to the Czar explaining his intention to take the offensive about a fortnight hence; and Blucher only a few days before had sent word to his wife that the Allies would soon enter France, for if they waited where they were for another year, Bonaparte would never attack them. Yet the very next day, June 16th, at Ligny, Bonaparte hurled himself like a thunderbolt on Blucher, and three days after, Wellington, having rushed from the Brussels ballroom to the battlefield at Waterloo, there saved himself and Europe, "so as by fire."

The occasional surprises our troops have sustained in the Transvaal need not stagger us, however much they ruffle our national complacency. They are not the first we have had to face, and may possibly prove by no means the last; but it is at least some sort of solace to know that however often we were surprised during the last long lingering stages of the war, our men yet more frequently surprised their surprisers. Whilst I was still there in July 1901, there were brought into Pretoria the surviving members of the Executive of the late Orange Free State, all notable men, all caught in their night-dresses—President Steyn alone escaping in shirt and pants; whilst his entire bodyguard, consisting of sixty burghers, were at the same time sent as prisoners to Bloemfontein. Laager after laager during those weary months was similarly surprised, and wagons and oxen and horses beyond all counting were captured, till apparently scarcely a horse or hoof or pair of heels was left on all the far-reaching *veldt*. The Boers resolutely chose ruin rather than surrender, and so, alas, the ruin came; for many, ruin beyond all remedy!

During this same period of despairing resistance the Boers imparted to the practice of train wrecking the finish of a fine art. At first they confined their attentions to troop trains, which are presumably lawful game; and as I was returning from Koomati Poort the troop train that immediately followed that on which I travelled was thus thrown off the rails near Pan, and about twenty of the Coldstream Guards, by whose side I had tramped for so many months, were killed or severely injured. The provision trains on which not the soldiers only, but the Boers' own wives and children, depended for daily food, were wrecked, looted or set on fire. Finally, they took to dynamiting ordinary passenger trains, and robbed of their personal belongings helpless women, including nursing sisters.

In Pretoria, I had the privilege of conversing with a cultured and godly lady who told me that she had been twice wrecked on her one journey up from the coast, and that the wrecking was as usual of a fatal type though fortunately not for her. Like one of the ironies of fate seemed the fact, of which she further informed me, that she had brought with her from England some hundreds of pounds' worth of bodily comforts, and yet more abounding spiritual consolations for free distribution among the wives and children of the very men who thus in one single journey had twice placed her life in deadly peril.

Among the Bush *Veldt* Carabineers at Pietersburg I found an engine-driver who in the course of a few months had thus been shot at and shattered by Boer drivers till he grew so sick of it that he threw up a situation worth £30 a month and joined the Fighting Scouts by way of finding some less perilous vocation. On the Sunday I spent there I worshipped with the Gordons who had survived the siege of Ladysmith; the day following as I returned to Pretoria, the train I travelled by was thrice ineffectually sniped; but soon after the turn of these same Gordons came to escort a train on that same line when nearly every man among them was killed or wounded, including their officer, and a sergeant with whom during that visit I had bowed in private prayer; but the driver, stoker and guard were deliberately led aside and shot after capture in cold blood. So my friend in the Carabineers had not long to wait for the justifying of his strange choice. Not until Norman William had planted stout Norman castles at every commanding point could he complete the conquest of our Motherland; and not until sturdy little block-houses sprang up thick and fast beside 5000 miles of rail and road was travelling in the Transvaal robbed of its worst peril, and the subjugation of the country made complete.

The worst of all our railway smashes, however, occurred close to Pretoria, and was caused by what seemed a bit of criminal carelessness, which resulted in a terrific collision. A Presbyterian chaplain who was in the damaged train showed me his battered and broken travelling trunk; but close beside the wreckage I saw the more terribly broken bodies of nine brave men awaiting burial. It was a tragedy too exquisitely distressing to be here described.

When the two Republics were formally annexed to the British Crown all the women and children scattered far and wide over the interminable *veldt*, were made British subjects by the very act; and from that hour for their support and safety the British Government became responsible. Yet all ordinary traffic by road or rail had long been stopped. All country stores were speedily cleared and closed. All farm stock or produce was gathered up and carried off, first by one set of hungry belligerents, then by the others; physic was still more scarce than food, and prowling bands of blacks or whites intensified the peril. The creation of huge concentration camps, all within easy reach of some railway, thus became an urgent necessity. No such prodigious enterprise could be carried through its initial stages without hardships having to be endured by such vast hosts of refugees, hardships only less severe than those the troops themselves sustained.

What I saw of these camps at Heidelberg, Barberton, and elsewhere made me wonder that so much had been done, and so well done; but a gentle lady sent from England to look for faults and flaws, and who was lovingly doing her best to find them, complained to me that all the tents were not quite sound, which I can quite believe. Canvas that is in constant use won't last for ever, and it is quite conceivable that at the end of a two years' campaign some of the tents in use were visibly the worse for wear. Thousands of our soldiers, however, went for a while without tents of any sort, while the families of their foes were being thus carefully sheltered in such tents as could then be procured. It is, moreover, in some measure reassuring to remember that the winter weather here is almost perfect, not a solitary shower falling for weeks together, and that within these tents were army blankets both thick and plentiful.

Complaint was also made in my presence that mutton, and yet again mutton, and only mutton, was supplied to the refugee camps by way of fresh meat rations, and that, moreover, a whole carcase, being mostly skin and bone, sometimes weighed only about twelve pounds. It is quite true that the scraggy Transvaal sheep would be looked down on and despised by their fat and far-famed English cousins, especially at that season of the year when the *veldt* is as bare and barren as the Sahara; but it surely is no fault of the British Government that not a green blade can anywhere be seen during these long rainless months, and that consequently all the flocks look famished. South African mutton is, at the best of times, a by no means dainty dish to set before a king, much less before the wife of a belligerent Boer; but British officers and men had to feed upon it and be content.

That no fresh beef, however, was by any chance supplied sounded to me quite a new charge, and set me enquiring as to its accuracy. I therefore wrote to one of the meat contractors, whom I personally knew as a man of specially good repute, and in reply was informed that for seven months he had regularly supplied the refugee camp in his neighbourhood with fresh beef as well as mutton, neither being always prime, he said, but the best that in war time the *veldt* could be made to yield! Those who hunt for grievances at a time like this can always find them, though when weighed in the balances they may perchance prove even lighter than Transvaal sheep.

It is undeniable that the child mortality in these refugee camps has been high compared with the average that prevails in a healthy English town. But the South African average, especially during the fever season, usually reaches quite another figure. A Hollander predikant, whom I found among our prisoners, told me that he, his wife, and his three children were all down with fever, but were without physic, and almost without food, when the English found them in the low country beyond Pietersburg, and brought them into camp. Nearly all their neighbours were in the same sad plight, and several died before they could be moved. In that and similar cases the camp mortality was bound to be high, but it takes a free-tongued Britisher to assert that it was the fault of the ever brutal British. In some camps there was an epidemic of measles, which occasionally occurs even in the happy homeland; but in the least sanitary refugee camp the mortality was never so high as in some of our own military fever camps, where the epidemic raged like a plague, and for many a weary week refused to be stayed. It should be remembered also that all the healthy manhood of the country was either still out on commando or in the overseas camps provided for our prisoners of war. The men brought in as refugees were only those who had no fight left in them—the halt, the maimed, the blind, the sick of every sort, the bent by extreme old age, the dying. I was startled by the specimens I saw. Here were gathered all the frailnesses and infirmities of two Republics; and to test an improvised camp of such a class by the standards which we rightly apply to an average English town is as misleading as it is mischievous.

When voyaging on the *Nubia* with the Scots Guards they often laughingly assured me it was the merest *walkover* that awaited us, and so in due time we discovered it to be. But it was a walk over well nigh the whole of South Africa, especially for these Scots. While during the second year of the war the Grenadiers were doing excellent work, chiefly in the northern part of Cape Colony, and the Coldstreams were similarly employed mainly along the lines of communication in the Orange River Colony, the Scots Guards trekked north, south, east and west. As a mere matter of mileage but much more as a matter of endurance they broke all previous records.

I have more than once written so warmly in praise of the daring and endurance of these men as to make me fear my words might for that very reason be heavily discounted. I was therefore delighted to find in Julian Ralph's *At Pretoria* a kindred eulogy:

> When I passed through the camps of the Grenadiers, Scots, and Coldstream Guards the other day, I thought I never saw men more wretchedly and pitifully circumstanced. The officers are the drawing-room pets of London society, which in large measure they rule. . . . Well, there they were on the *veldt* looking like a lot of half drowned rats, as indeed they had been ever since the cold season and the rains had set in. You would not like to see a vagabond dog fare as they were doing. They had no tents. They could get no dry wood to make fires with. They were soaked to the bone night and day, and they stood about in mud toe-deep. Titled and untitled alike all were in the same scrape, and all were stoutly insisting that it didn't matter; it was all in the game.

During this second period of the war the staying powers of the Irregulars was no less severely tested. Here and there there was a momentary failure, but as a whole the men did superbly. Multitudes of the Colonials, who on completing their first term of service, returned to Australia, New Zealand, or Canada, actually re-enlisted for a second term, and in several cases paid their own passage to the Cape in order to rejoin. The Colonials are incomparably keener Imperialists than we ourselves claim to be. Some of the officers of these Irregular troops were themselves of a most irregular type, and in the case of town, or mine, or cattle, Guards were occasionally chosen, not with reference to any martial fitness they might possess, but because of their knowledge of and influence over the men they now commanded, and previously in civilian life had probably employed. One of these called his men to "fall in—*two thick!*" and another, when he wanted to halt his Guards, is reported to have thrown up his arms and said, "*Whoa!* Stop!" None need wonder if troops so handled sometimes found themselves in a tight corner. Yet of these newly recruited Irregulars, as of the most staid Reservists, there was good reason to be proud; and as concerning his own Irregulars in the Peninsular War Wellington said that with them he could go anywhere or do anything, so were these also as a whole entitled to similar confidence and to a similar tribute.

How fully these citizen soldiers hazarded their lives for the empire every cemetery in South Africa bears sad and silent witness, including the one I know so well in Pretoria. Indeed that particular burial-place is to me the most pathetic spot on earth, and enshrines in striking fashion the whole history of the Transvaal, whereof only one or two illustrations can here be given. In a tiny walled enclosure—a cemetery within a cemetery—filled with the soldier victims of our earlier wars, I found a slab whereon was this inscription:

To the memory of
Corporal Henry Watson
Who died at Pretoria 17th May 1877; aged 25 years.
He was the first British soldier to give up his life
in the service of his country, *on the annexation*
of the Transvaal Republic!

Nearby on another slab I read:

In loving memory of
John Mitchell Elliott Aged 37
Captain and Paymaster of the 94th Regiment,
Who was killed for Queen and Country while crossing
the Vaal River on the night of Dec. 29th, 1880.

There, too, I found one other slab which recorded in this strange style the closing of a most ignoble chapter in our imperial history:

This Cemetery was planted,
and the graves left in good repair,
by the men of the Royal Scots Fusiliers,
prior to the evacuation of Pretoria, 1881.

Two brief decades rush away, and once again that same cemetery opens wide its gates to welcome new battalions of British
soldiers, each of whom like his forerunner of 1877 *gave up his life
in the service of his country*; but these late-comers represent every
province and almost every hamlet of a far-reaching empire, as
well as every branch of the service; while over all and applicable
to all alike is the epitaph on the tomb of the Hampshire Volunteers, *We answered duty's call!*

The Dutch section of that cemetery also witnessed some
sensational scenes during the period now referred to.

On July 20th Mrs Kruger, the ex-President's wife, died, and as
one of a prodigious crowd I attended her homely funeral. She was
herself well-nigh the homeliest woman in Pretoria, and one of the
most illiterate; but precisely because she was content to be her simple God-fearing self, put on no airs, and intermeddled not in matters beyond her ken, she was universally respected and regretted.

During this second period of the war the troops in Pretoria
continued to justify Lord Roberts' description of them as "the
best-behaved army in the world." The Sunday evening services in Wesley Church were always crowded with them, and the
nightly meetings held in the S.A.G.M. marquees were not only
wonderfully well attended but were also marked by much spiritual power. Pretoria, after we took possession of it, witnessed
many a tear, and occasional tragedies; but it was in Pretoria I
heard a young Canadian soldier sing the following song, which
aptly illustrates the type of life to which many a trooper has
more or less fully attained during this South African campaign:

I'm walking close to Jesus' side,
So close that I can hear
The softest whispers of His love
In fellowship so dear,
And feel His great Almighty hand

Protects me in this hostile land.
Oh wondrous bliss, oh joy sublime,
I've Jesus with me all the time!

I'm leaning on His loving breast
Along life's weary way;
My path illumined by His smiles
Grows brighter day by day;
No foes, no woes, my heart can fear
With my Almighty Friend so near.
Oh wondrous bliss, oh joy sublime,
I've Jesus with me all the time!

CHAPTER 16

Pretoria and the Royal Family

During the next few months many events occurred in Pretoria of vital interest to the whole empire, and especially to the various members of the Royal Family. To these this seems the fittest place to refer, though most of them took place during my various return visits to Pretoria, and are therefore not precisely ranged in due chronologic order.

It was an ever memorable scene I witnessed in the Kirk Square when the Union Jack was once more formally hoisted in the midst of armed men, a miscellaneous crowd of cheering civilians, and an important group of Basuto chiefs who had been specially invited to witness the ceremonious annexation of the conquered territory and to hear proclaimed the Royal pleasure that the erstwhile South African Republic should henceforth be known by the new, yet older, title of The Transvaal.

So came to an end the Queen's Suzerainty—an ill-omened term, which had proved fruitful in all conceivable kinds of misinterpretation, and made possible the misunderstandings and controversies that culminated in this cruel and wasteful war. So was resumed the Queen's Sovereignty, which as subsequent events proved, ought never to have been renounced; and so too was made plain the way for that ultimate federation of all South Africa, under one glorious flag, for which Lord Carnarvon and Sir Bartle Frere long years before had laboured apparently in vain. This fresh unfurling of that flag was a pledge of equal liberties alike for Boer and Briton, as well as of fair play to the natives. It was a guarantee that the *Pax Britannica* would henceforth be maintained from the Zambezi to the Cape, and that in this vast area, well nigh as large as all Europe, there would be nursed into matureness and majestic strength, a new Anglo-Saxon nation, essentially Christian, essentially liberty-loving, and rivalling in wealth, in enterprise and prowess, the ripest promise of united Canada, and newly federated Australia.

In this Imperial conflict the heroic fashion in which both those Commonwealths rallied for the defence of our Imperial flag is one of the most hopeful facts in modern history. "Waterloo," said Wellington, "did more than any other battle I know of toward the true object of all battles—the peace of the world."

A similar comment both by victors and vanquished may possibly hereafter be made concerning this deplorable Boer war. But that can come to pass only provided we as a united people strive to cherish more fully the spirit embodied in Kipling's *Diamond Jubilee Recessional*:

God of our fathers, known of old,—
Lord of our far-flung battle-line,—
Beneath Whose awful Hand we hold
Dominion over palm and pine,—
Lord God of Hosts, be with us yet,
Lest we forget—lest we forget!

★ ★ ★

For heathen heart that puts her trust
In reeking tube and iron shard—
All valiant dust that builds on dust,
And guarding calls not Thee to guard,—
For frantic boast and foolish word,
Thy mercy on Thy people, Lord!—
Amen.

To Dr Macgregor the Queen is reported to have said at Balmoral in November 1900, "My heart bleeds for these terrible losses. The war lies heavy on my heart." And Lord Wantage assures us that her Majesty's very last words, spoken only a few weeks later, were "Oh that peace may come!" Both assertions may well find credence; so characteristic are they of her whom all men revered and loved. As the head and representative of the whole empire, every bereavement caused by the war had in it for her a kind of personal element. But her sympathies and sufferings were destined to become more than merely vicarious. As in connection with one of our petty West African wars she was compelled to mourn the death of Prince Henry of Battenberg, so in the course of this South African war death again invaded her own immediate circle. The griefs that hastened her end were strongly personal as well as representative, and so made her all the more the true representative of those she ruled.

It was in the early days of that dull November, tidings reached her and us of the dangerous illness of Prince Christian Victor. Not alone in name was he Christian; and not alone in name was he Victor. On the voyage out, in the *Braemar Castle*, through the absence of a chaplain, the prince conducted divine worship with the troops. One of our best appointed hospital trains was *The Princess Christian Victor*, so called presumably because provided by the bounty of his and her princely hands and hearts. He was what Sir Ascelin declared "The last of the English" to be—"A very perfect knight, beloved and honoured of all men."

It therefore alarmed both town and camp to learn that enteric, the deadliest of all a soldier's foes, had claimed him, like so many a lowlier man, for its prey, and that his life was in mortal peril. At that time he was a patient in the Imperial Yeomanry Hospital which consisted of Mr T. W. Beckett's beautiful mansion, and a formidable array of tents that almost covered the whole of the extensive grounds. Here prince and private alike reaped the fruit of the lavish beneficence which provided and maintained this magnificent hospital. All that wealth could procure was there of skill and tenderness, and such appliances as the healing art requires. All was there, except the power to command success. With what seemed startling suddenness the prince's vital powers collapsed, and the half masting of flags, far and wide, told to friend and foe the tidings of the Queen's irreparable loss.

It was at first proposed that the body of the prince should be taken to England for interment, and certain companies of the Grenadiers, to which battalion I was still attached, were detailed for escort duty, but finally it was decided all fittingly that

Part of I.Y. Hospital in the grounds surrounding Mr T. W. Beckett's mansion at Pretoria

he should be laid to rest in the city where he fell, and among the comrades who like him had laid down life in defence of Queen and duty. So Pretoria witnessed a stately funeral, the like of which South Africa had never seen before, as the Queen's own kinsman was borne, by the martial representatives of the whole empire, to the quiet cemetery which this war had so enlarged and so enriched.

Disease and fatal woundings combined cost us in this strangely protracted conflict, scarcely more lives than the one great fight at Waterloo, where on the English side alone 15,000 fell,—for the most part to rise no more. In this South African war, up to January 31st, 1901, about 7700 of our men had died of disease; 700 by accidents; and 4300 of wounds. But this Pretoria cemetery like that at Bloemfontein, where 1500 interments took place in less than fifteen months, affords striking testimony to the common loyalty of all classes throughout the empire. Volunteers belonging to the Imperial Light Horse, raised exclusively in South Africa here lie, side by side, with volunteers belonging to the Imperial Yeomanry, raised exclusively in England. Sons of the empire, from Canadian Vancouver and Australian Victoria, here find a common sepulchre. The soldier prince whose dwelling was in king's palaces here becomes, as in the conflict of the battlefield so in the quiet of a hero's grave, a comrade of the private soldier whose dwelling was a cottage; and be it noted, the death of the lowliest may involve quite as much of heartbreak as the lordliest.

At the close of a simple military funeral in this same cemetery, the orderly in charge came to me and said, "I never felt so much over any case. This grave means four orphans left to the care of an invalid mother. I knew the man well, and he was always scheming what to do for his family when he got back: but *this* is the end of it!"

That dead soldier was merely a private. Not one of his own particular comrades was present, but only the necessary fatigue party. No flag was flung over his coffin, no bugle sounded "the last post." No tear was shed. It was only a commonplace *casualty*, one among thousands. But it was a tragedy all the same. These tragedies in humble life seldom find a trumpeter; but they are none the less terrible on that account; and if half the truth were known and realised concerning the horrors and heartbreak caused by war, all Christendom would clamour for its speedy superseding by honest Courts of Arbitration.

I was still in Pretoria when tidings arrived concerning the illness and death of the Queen; and was present in that same Kirk Square when King Edward VII. was proclaimed "Overlord of the Transvaal." In connection with the former event a memorial service, at which the military were largely represented, was held in Wesley Church on Sunday, January 27th. The Rev. Geo. Weavind, as well as Rev. H. W. Goodwin, took part in the proceedings, and I was privileged to deliver the following address which may serve to illustrate, once for all, the type of teaching given to the troops throughout this campaign:

I bowed down mourning as one that bewaileth his mother
—Ps. xxxv. 14

As there is no relationship on earth so imperishably true and tender as that between a mother and her children, so also there is no mourning on earth so real and reverent as that beside a mother's grave. This saying therefore of the Psalmist describes with exquisite exactness our common attitude today; and voices, as scarcely any other single sentence could, our profoundest thought and feeling. We behold at this hour a many peopled empire bowed down mourning; and almost all other nations sharing in our sorrows; but it is not over the death of a mere monarch, however mighty, the whole earth thus feels moved to unfeigned lamentation.

It is the death of the representative Mother of our race and age that bids us wrap our mourning robes around us. For any record of such another we ransack in vain the treasure stores of all history. She is the only mother that ever reigned in her own right over any potent realm; and certainly over our own. Queen Mary of unhappy memory, died childless, and her more fortunate sister, "Good Queen Bess," went down to her grave a maiden queen; but in the case of Victoria, four sons and five daughters found their earliest cradle in her queenly arms. She is said to have been in almost all respects as capable as the ablest of

215

Wesleyan Church and Manse, Pretoria

her predecessors, and was even to extreme old age unsparingly devoted to the discharge of her royal duties. Yet not by reason of her laboriousness, her linguistic gifts, or gifts of statesmanship will she be longest and most lovingly remembered. Put it on record, as her chief glory, that in her own person she honoured family life and kept it pure, when for generations such pureness had seldom been suffered to show its face. Her most popular portraits represent her as the centre of a group of her own children, grandchildren and great-grandchildren—a chain of living royalties reaching to the fourth generation. It was never so seen in Israel before; and thus have been linked to the throne of England by potent blood bonds almost all the Protestant royalties of Europe. The Queen retained to the last a heart that was young, because to the last she lived in tenderest relationship to the young. I cannot therefore even imagine a more beautifully appropriate or suggestive message than that by which the new King conveyed to the Lord Mayor of London, tidings of the great Queen's death:

> My beloved Mother passed peacefully away, at 6.30, surrounded by her children and grandchildren.

In the midst of her children she lived; and all fittingly in the midst of her children she died!

As her most signal virtues were of the domestic type, so also her acutest sorrows were domestic. A father's strongly tender love, or wisely-watchful care, she never knew. In one sad year there was taken from her her long-widowed mother, and her almost idolized husband, Albert the Good.

> *Who reverenced his conscience as his king;*
> *Whose glory was redeeming human wrong;*
> *Who spake no slander, no, nor listened to it;*
> *. . . . thro' all the tract of years,*
> *Wearing the white flower of a blameless life.*

Concerning that great sorrow, the Queen was wont in homely phrase to say that it made so large a hole in her heart, all other sorrows dropped lightly through. Nevertheless of other sorrows too she was called to bear no common share. As you are all well aware, two of the daughters of our widowed Queen have themselves long been widows. Two of her sons perished in their ripening prime. Her favourite daughter, the Princess Alice, and her favourite grandson, the heir-presumptive to her throne, drooped beside her like flowers untimely touched by frost; and within the last few weeks we ourselves have seen yet another of her grandsons laid beneath the sod in this very city of Pretoria. Nor is it with absolutely unqualified regret we call to mind that notably sad event. Like many another of lowlier name he died in the service of his queen—and ours; and perchance the Queen herself rebelled, not as against an utterly unfitting thing, when thus called in her own person to share the griefs of those among her own people, whom recent events have made so desolate.

Reverentially we may venture to say that in all afflictions she was afflicted, and thus endeared herself to those she ruled as no other monarch ever did. Because she was Queen of Sorrows she became also Queen of Hearts.

That of which we have just spoken was indeed her last sore bereavement; and now that to her who shed such countless tears there has come the end of all grief, we have therewith witnessed the full and final prevailings of her Laureate's familiar prayer—

May all love His love unseen, but felt, o'ershadow thee;
The love of all thy sons encompass thee,
The love of all thy daughters cherish thee,
The love of all thy people comfort thee:
Till God's love set thee at his side again.

The day she ceased to breathe was to her as a new, a nobler bridal day. The wife has found her long-lost consort; the mother is at home!

Queen Victoria was not merely a model mother in the narrow circle of her own household. She was emphatically the mother of her people—a people multitudinous as the stars of the midnight sky. One fourth of the inhabitants of the entire globe gladly submitted to her gentle sway. The vastest sovereignties of the ancient world were mere satrapies compared with the length and breadth of her domain, and today east, west, north and south bow down beneath a common sorrow beside her bier. In synagogue and mosque and temple, in kirk and church of every class and creed, men render thanks for one "who wrought her people lasting good," and humbly own before their God that

A thousand claims to reverence closed
In her, as mother, wife, and queen.

Almost as a matter of course this monarch and mother of many nations became more and more liberal-minded and large-hearted. For her to have become a bigot would have been a very miracle of perverseness. She rejoiced in all true progress in all places, and made the sorrows of the whole world her own. Famine in the East Indies, or a desolating hurricane in the West, called forth from her an instant telegram of queenly sympathy or, it may be, a queenly gift. Every effort for the betterment of her people awoke her liveliest interest. The east end of London, only less well than the west, was known to her. From Windsor to Woolwich she recently went in midwinter, that with her own hand she might distribute flowers among her wounded soldiers, and with her own lips speak to them words of solace. At that same inclement season she crossed the Irish Channel to show her vulnerable face once more among her Irish people, and I should not marvel if for such a queen some would even dare to die!

It was ever with the simplicity of a sister of the people rather than with the symbolic splendours of a sovereign, she went in and out among us. In the full pomp and pageantry of her high position she seemed to find no special pleasure. Even on Jubilee Day, when her presence crowned the superbest procession England ever saw, she looked immeasurably more like a mighty mother of her martial sons than like a majestic monarch in the midst of her exulting subjects. Filial love and filial loyalty that day reached their climax. Till then the best informed knew not how truly she was the mother of us all!

Her prodigious hold upon the hearts of her people was largely due to the unexampled length of her reign.

That she ever reigned is one of the many marvels of divine mercy found in the history of our native land. Note that her father was not the first, but the fourth son of old King George III.;

that the three elder sons all died childless, and that her own father died within a few months of her birth. Victoria seems to have been as truly a special gift of God to England as Samuel was to Israel. This longest of all reigns was unmarred by any break of any kind from first to last. Had our princess come to the throne only a few months earlier a regency must have been proclaimed, and had she lingered a few months longer increasing infirmities might have forced that same calamity upon us. But through God's mercy hers was a full orbed reign. There was no abdication of her power for a single day. The first serious illness of her life was also her last, and to her it was granted to cease at once to work and live.

So long ago as September 1852, when her devoted friend and adviser, the famous Duke of Wellington, died, she pathetically said "I shall soon stand sadly alone"; then naming one after another of her recent intimates she added "They are all gone!" That of necessity became increasingly true in the course of the remaining half century of her life. Not one among the many friends of her youth remained at her side amid the deepening shadows of her eventide. Surrounded by new acquaintances and new kinships a loneliness was hers, which few of us are ever likely in any similar measure to experience.

Every throne in Europe except her own has witnessed repeated changes in the course of her strangely eventful career, sometimes as the result of appalling revolutions and sometimes as the fruit of a dastardly assassin's dagger; but amid all He who was Abraham's shield and exceeding great reward deigned to compass our Queen with songs of deliverance. Never was any monarch so much prayed for; and that she may long reign over us is a petition that in special measure has prevailed. Not three score years and ten, but four score years and two, have been the days of the years of her life, and now that the inevitable end has come, no voice of complaining is heard in our streets. Such a death we commemorate with thankful song!

The Queen's whole reign was frankly based on the fear of God; and to find such in English history I fear we shall have to travel back a full thousand years to the days of Alfred the Great, who was also Alfred the Good, and whose favourite saying was—

Come what may come,
God's will be welcome!

When Victoria was still a girl of fifteen she was solemnly confirmed in the Chapel Royal, and in her case that impressive service manifestly meant—what alas, it does not always imply—a life henceforth wholly given to God.

At two o'clock in the morning of June 21st, 1837, she was roused from her slumbers in old Kensington Palace, and hastily flinging a shawl over her nightdress, she presently stood in the presence of the Lord Chamberlain and the Archbishop of Canterbury, to learn from their lips that her royal uncle had given up the ghost, and that she, a trembling maid of just eighteen, was Queen. Thereupon, so we are told, her eyes filled with tears, her lips quivered, and turning to the Archbishop she said, "Pray for me!" So that instant all three lowly bowed imploring heaven's help. The Queen began her reign upon her knees. Her first act of conscious royalty was thus to render heartfelt homage to "The Prince of the kings of the earth." Hence came it to pass—

Her court was pure, her life sincere.

Her favourite recreations were consequently not those provided by the ballroom, the card-table, the racecourse, or even the theatre. Music, the simple charms of country life, and, manifold ministries of mercy, were the pastimes that became her best; and she never appeared in the eyes of her people more truly royal than when seen sitting by the bedside of a Highland cottager, reading to the sick out of God's own Gospel the wonderful words of life.

We are here at liberty to use a scriptural phrase and to add that she "married in the Lord." Royal etiquette required that the Queen should herself select the lover destined to share the pleasures and responsibilities of her high position, and her choice fell not on one renowned for gaiety, for wealth or wit, but on one in whom she recognised the double gift of abounding good sense and the grace of our Lord Jesus Christ. For a choice so supremely wise, and for a marriage so supremely happy, all thoughtful Englishmen still render thanks to God.

Her piety was as broad as it was deep and practical. The head of the Anglican Church, when in England she worshipped with Anglicans only; but when in Scotland she no less regularly repaired to the Presbyterian Kirk, and only a few months ago gave expression to her warm appreciation of the work done for God and man by "The people called Methodists." She would tolerate no intolerance in things pertaining to godliness, and on her Jubilee Day insisted that all creeds should be invited to join in one common act of worship. For that reason among others the Queen required that historic service should be held in the open air, on the steps, it is true, of our stateliest cathedral; but none the less under God's own arching sky, which makes the whole earth a temple. We owe not a little of our religious liberty to the personal influence and example of our much lamented Queen; and we, therefore, show ourselves worthy to have been her subjects, only when we shun utterly all indifference concerning things divine, yet give no place to bigotry; when we seek out not the worst, but the best, in every man, and honestly strive to make the best of that best.

With the new century we suddenly find ourselves subjects of a new Sovereign, and with equal sincerity, if not with equal fervour, we say, "God save the King." May his reign also like that of his predecessor bring blessing to many lands! We crave not for him, and seek not in him, unexampled greatness. We desire chiefly that he may "love mercy, do justly, and walk humbly with his God." His rich legacy of newly-created loyalty he will thus assuredly retain and augment.

It is commonly said that this new century, like the last, has begun with a notable lack of notable men, but, nevertheless, never yet have we been left without trusty leaders in the hour of national necessity; and as it has been so will it be!

We thank Thee, Lord, when Thou hast need,
The man aye ripens for the deed!

Yet the new century clamours importunately, not so much for great men, as for good men. All greatness perishes that is not broad based on godliness. The best gift for this new era that God Himself can bestow upon our people, is the grace of deep-toned repentance, an impassioned love of righteousness, a never flinching resolve to walk in newness of life; for then will the brightness of even the Victorian era be splendidly outshone, and heaven itself will hasten to make all things new. We who believe in Christ have learned to say:

Oh Thou bleeding Lamb
The true morality is love of Thee!

Along that same path of love divine lies also the truest patriotism and the speediest perfecting of our national life. I pray you, therefore, let the God of your late Queen be yet more completely your God; her Saviour your Saviour; and make this Memorial Service doubly memorable by bowing this moment at His feet, "In full and glad surrender."

On Saturday, March 22nd, 1902, Schalk Burger, late State-Secretary Reitz, and General Lucas Meyer are reported to have appeared in Pretoria, presumably with a view to the submission of those they represent to the sovereign authority of our new King, whose approaching Coronation, Pretoria, even while I write, is preparing to celebrate with unexampled splendour. It is intended to break all previous festival records, and some of the Guards may only too probably still be there to share therein. But that is quite another story, and must find for itself quite another historian. Meanwhile—

God send His people peace!

LEONAUR

ALSO FROM LEONAUR

AVAILABLE IN SOFTCOVER OR HARDCOVER WITH DUST JACKET

DOING OUR 'BIT' *by Ian Hay*—Two Classic Accounts of the Men of Kitchener's 'New Army' During the Great War including *The First 100,000* & *All In It*.

AN EYE IN THE STORM by *Arthur Ruhl*—An American War Correspondent's Experiences of the First World War from the Western Front to Gallipoli and Beyond.

STAND & FALL by *Joe Cassells*—A Soldier's Recollections of the 'Contemptible Little Army' and the Retreat from Mons to the Marne, 1914.

RIFLEMAN MACGILL'S WAR by *Patrick MacGill*—A Soldier of the London Irish During the Great War in Europe including *The Amateur Army, The Red Horizon* & *The Great Push*.

WITH THE GUNS by *C. A. Rose & Hugh Dalton*—Two First Hand Accounts of British Gunners at War in Europe During World War 1- Three Years in France with the Guns and With the British Guns in Italy.

EAGLES OVER THE TRENCHES by *James R. McConnell & William B. Perry*—Two First Hand Accounts of the American Escadrille at War in the Air During World War 1-Flying For France: With the American Escadrille at Verdun and Our Pilots in the Air.

THE BUSH WAR DOCTOR by *Robert V. Dolbey*—The Experiences of a British Army Doctor During the East African Campaign of the First World War.

THE 9TH—THE KING'S (LIVERPOOL REGIMENT) IN THE GREAT WAR 1914 - 1918 by *Enos H. G. Roberts*—Like many large cities, Liverpool raised a number of battalions in the Great War. Notable among them were the Pals, the Liverpool Irish and Scottish, but this book concerns the wartime history of the 9th Battalion – The Kings.

THE GAMBARDIER by *Mark Severn*—The experiences of a battery of Heavy artillery on the Western Front during the First World War.

FROM MESSINES TO THIRD YPRES by *Thomas Floyd*—A personal account of the First World War on the Western front by a 2/5th Lancashire Fusilier.

THE IRISH GUARDS IN THE GREAT WAR - VOLUME 1 by *Rudyard Kipling*—Edited and Compiled from Their Diaries and Papers Volume 1 The First Battalion.

THE IRISH GUARDS IN THE GREAT WAR - VOLUME 2 by *Rudyard Kipling*—Edited and Compiled from Their Diaries and Papers Volume 2 The Second Battalion.

www.ingramcontent.com/pod-product-compliance
Lightning Source LLC
Chambersburg PA
CBHW032052080426
42733CB00006B/245